Paul Kenyon

Op[illegible] Cabinet

The Inside Story

This first edition published in 2020

ISBN 9781838535049

Published by Discovery Publications UK
www.discoverypublications.co.uk

Cover design and illustrations by Peapod Studios Scotland
www.peapodstudios.co.uk

This book is dedicated to the memory of

Detective Chief Inspector John Ralphson.

1921 – 2016

Contents

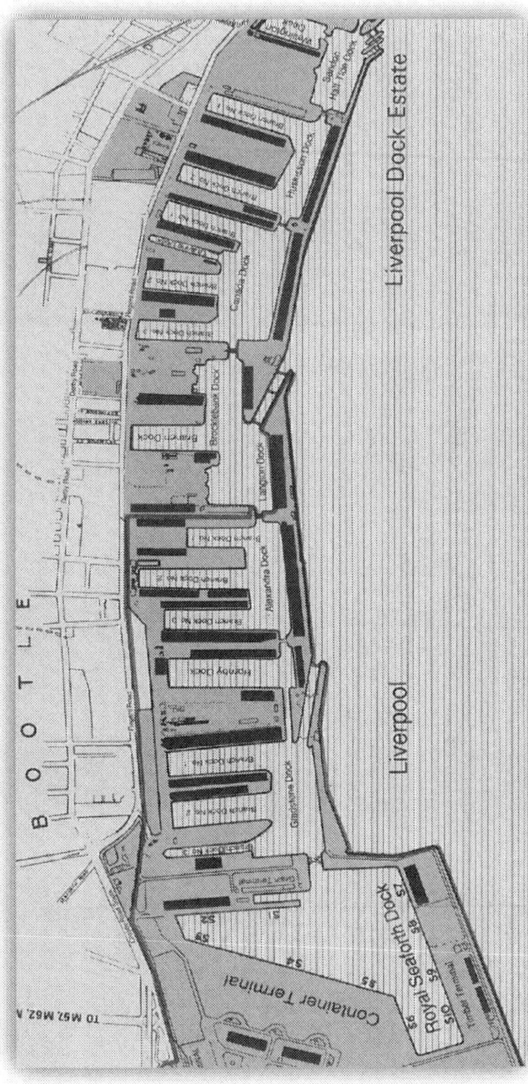
Liverpool Dock Estate
Liverpool
BOOTLE
Royal Seaforth Dock
Container Terminal
Langton Dock
Alexandra Dock
Gladstone Dock
Canada Dock
Brocklebank Dock
Huskisson Dock
Hornby Dock

Acknowledgements

I would first of all like to thank those officers I had the privilege to work with on this operation and the assistance they gave whether it was for days, weeks or as in some cases, years. Most of all John Ralphson Det. Ch. Insp. (R.I.P), Jim Irvine, my Det. Ch. Supt. (R.I.P.) and Ken Candler, who initially helped me to find my feet in C.I.D. Bill Donaldson QPM. Chief Constable (R.I.P.) for agreeing to pursue this operation via the D.P.P.Especially, Rod Bradley who not only, like myself, dedicated himself to this enquiry, but became a good friend.

Also, the Dutch officers who assisted, Fred Bakker, Eef Krabbendam and others, together with Corporal John Boulton and his colleagues of the National Harbours Police, Vancouver, Canada.

My thanks also go to Shaun Rothwell for his assistance in the history of Liverpool Docks policing. To Lynne McGowan at Peapod Studios and also to Discovery Publications up in Scotland for their patience and advice.

My friends and family, past and present, who I neglected whilst working on this enquiry. And last but not least I must thank my wife for suffering with me, whilst writing this book.

A percentage of any profit from the sale of this book will be donated to the British Transport Police Welfare Fund and the North West Police Benevolent Fund.

Thank you all.

Foreword

At the end of 1979, several Police Forces throughout Europe were confronted with the large-scale thefts of currency which were taking place on board vessels docked in seaports.

Thefts on board vessels was nothing out of the common but now large amounts of money disappeared from the Captains cabins, stolen from safes, without any signs of breaking or forced entry.

In Amsterdam, a lot of reports were received at the offices of the River Police. We did not have any clue how this was happening. It was a complete grope in the dark until the Port of Liverpool Police made contact with de C.I.D. department of the River Police of Rotterdam. This phone call was at the beginning of a long term, unique C.I.D. investigation throughout Europe.

The Operation, code named Cabinet, brought a lot of Police officers especially from Liverpool, Amsterdam and Rotterdam together.

In Liverpool, the gang of known criminals that were suspected of being responsible for these thefts, the working methods of this gang was impertinent, skilful, quick and refined.
In this book, my good English friend, Paul Kenyon, explains absolutely clearly what happened and how it happened. An absolute good judge of C.I.D. work.
It stands to reading, that a lot of frustrations passed by, when arrested criminals were released from custody again

and again through lack of witnesses at court. The thefts went on! Rather frustrating indeed, but gave the responsible Police officers the perseverance to continue all the time. Operation Cabinet started and grew.

Because it was known that the suspects came from Liverpool and visited Amsterdam C.I.D. information was exchanged all the time and enquiries made enthusiastically.
The criminal acts, of course were reported to the Amsterdam public prosecutor, he gave us full co-operation and judicial support in this case. The public prosecutor in Rotterdam assisted as well. Co-operation from these was essential and required under Dutch law.
The River Police of the National Police Force at Amsterdam became the co-ordination centre.
It was a truly unique investigation, both in the U.K. and Holland. Interpol gave support and many times Dutch and British Police officers saw each other either in the U.K. or Holland to discuss. The trap was placed, and a lot of officers involved.
Paul Kenyon made an outstanding achievement by writing this book and explains clearly what difficulties were faced
A unique investigation, I say it again, ... there will never be another like it!!

Reading this book is highly recommended.
JULY 2020
Fred Bakker
Former National Police Force, River Police Amsterdam Holland.
Commandant, Recherchegroep, Rijkspolitie, Amsterdam (Retired)

INTRODUCTION

Introduction

I will, first of all, endeavour to explain why it was necessary this Operation came about.

The Port of Liverpool has always been policed in some form or other.

There was the Liverpool Dock Police, formed in 1811, which existed until 1837.

The Liverpool City Police, formed in 1836, covered not only the city of Liverpool but the expanding dock system into Bootle, and coverage for that was funded by the Dock Company. In 1865 the River Mersey Police was formed; the constables being sworn in as Borough Constables and funded by the Mersey Dock and Harbour Company. This force was in existence until February 1920, when the officers were absorbed into Liverpool City Police. *(see Figure 1)*

Liverpool and Bootle Constabulary, created in 1967, was responsible for policing the whole of the Liverpool Docks. Due to local regional changes, in 1974 Merseyside Police was created, taking over the responsibility. Seaforth Dock, situated at the most northerly end of the dock system, had opened in 1972.

A similar situation had been in place in Birkenhead covering the docks there. Birkenhead Borough Police formed in 1836, later being absorbed into Cheshire Constabulary in 1967, then in 1974, due to the regional changes, Merseyside Police took over the responsibility of policing Birkenhead and Wallasey Docks.

In the early 1970s, due to high costs for policing being paid by The Mersey Dock and Harbour Company to Merseyside Police, it was decided to create a specific Police Force to cover the dock system on both sides of the River Mersey, the Liverpool and Birkenhead docks. So, through an Act of Parliament, the Port of Liverpool Police came into existence. The force's role was phased in through 1976, and by 1977 it was fully responsible for policing the entire docks system.

Thefts of money and valuables had always taken place from ships' cabins, whether it be by a prostitute going onboard a ship or an opportunist thief entering the dock estate and sneaking onboard.

The Police had always encountered problems when attempting to convict a perpetrator. The offenders soon realised that if they entered a plea of not guilty at court the case would be adjourned whilst a date was fixed for a trial, requiring the victim and any witnesses to attend court and give evidence. This posed a significant problem, as the trial date would most likely be at least a month away and the ship, together with the complainant/victim and any witnesses, would have long since departed. Trying to get the witnesses etc. back for any court case proved difficult, so the offenders walked away "scott free", with the prosecution having to withdraw all charges, offering no evidence.

In 1976/77 the amount of thefts from the ships' cabins had increased significantly, especially from Captains' cabins, where large amounts of cash were involved.

In order to combat these offences, "Operation Cabinet" came into being.

The reason I decided to write this book was to tell the story of how a small police force, through sheer determination, dedication and tenacity was able to bring about the arrest and conviction of a gang of international cabin thieves that had plundered their way throughout Europe and further afield.

The initial idea of writing this book was suggested to me by my then Detective Chief Superintendent, Jim Irvine, who upon his retirement advised me to write a book on the subject, saying to me, "Gather all the material you need when this is over and publish a book."

When I retired, John Ralphson, my Detective Chief Inspector, who figures throughout this book, advised the same and told me to take notes of everything that would be needed, saying (and I can recall his exact words), "Do that book, Paul, tell the story, it was a unique investigation and there'll never be another like it," advising me though, not to publish it for a few years; so I waited, and here it is.

Figure 1.

The Liverpool River Police, courtesy of Mr Tony McDevitt R.I.P, whose Grandfather Joseph Charles Duffy, second left back row, served with the River Police quite a number of years.
The photograph was taken in the old `Immigration` sheds at the Princes Landing stage, now demolished.

One

MY BACKGROUND

My Background

It was the Spring of 1971, I was nineteen years old, married with a young son, and had decided I needed a more secure job, with prospects, rather than having worked as a freelance photographer and mental health nurse.

My then brother in law Dave who was employed by British Rail told me about the Railway Police as he called them. I had considered joining the police in my last years at school, but photography had become my main interest. I had wanted to be a press photographer.

Following a little research, I discovered the Railway Police, that he referred to, were actually called the British Transport Police.

I made enquiries, filled in an application form, and the next thing a uniformed inspector visited me, interviewed me and shortly afterwards I was asked to attend the British Transport Police Divisional Police Office, Liverpool to sit an entrance exam.

There was only myself, sat in a small room, I wrote a short essay on what I had done since leaving school. Then a really nice Detective Sergeant who I will always remember, John Henry, asked me to read a passage from the morning's

Telegraph, oh yes, no *Daily Mirror* stuff, you know! I then completed a maths paper, quite simple stuff really.

After a short while (suppose they were checking to ensure I wasn't a complete numpty), I was given an envelope and told to attend at a doctor's surgery in Ranelagh Street (the Liverpool equivalent to Harley Street) for a medical.

I remember walking there (that was an experience, as a child I was always told, "You don't go to Liverpool, it's too rough"). Upon arrival and after presenting the letter, being given a quick examination, and waiting a short while, I was then handed a letter to take back.

Obviously, it had been decided that not only was I compos mentis but that I was a fit bastard too.

I was then asked to attend the Divisional Commander's office in Manchester on Friday of that week. I agreed and was given a rail pass and instructions.

Friday morning came, and off I went on the train to Manchester Piccadilly station and to the British Transport Police, Divisional Police HQ offices.

I was ushered into a room, where, there was a portly figure in a uniform sat behind a large desk.

He introduced himself as Chief Superintendent Steed, the Divisional Commander.

He was a nice guy, and he asked me a few questions. One was, "If you were walking down the street and saw someone throw a brick through a window, what would you do?"

Within a second, I knew what answer he wanted to hear. I replied, "Grab him and hope someone would call the police." He smiled and said, "Good answer," or words to that effect.

He told me all was OK; I was accepted and asked if I would like to start the following Monday. I thought, "Bloody hell this is happening rather fast." but agreed.

He went on to give me some advice. He told me that some of the older officers would tell me there were no prospects in the job and I would be better finding something else. That stuck in my mind and he was right, it did happen.

So, the following Monday morning I attended the British Transport Police Office at Lime Street Station, Liverpool. Firstly, I was introduced to the Duty Inspector, Sergeant then some of my colleagues.

A couple of days were spent in the radio room with a really nice old, uniformed bobby, P.C. Harry Pedder, observing how calls were taken, messages logged, and radio calls dealt with. That week myself and another new recruit Sandra Fairclough, were sworn in as Constables at Bootle Magistrates court.

Within a few days having been given a rail pass, I was on a train to London visiting a uniform supply company. They supplied the Metropolitan Police too. There I was measured up, and a week later had my uniform.

Having been rostered onto a shift pattern, I found myself doing nights, before attending the Police number one district training centre at Bruche, Warrington.

Whilst on nights I accompanied P.C. Phil White, who had in fact not long returned from Bruche himself. On the second night we locked up, nothing spectacular, the offence was obtaining a pecuniary advantage by deception, contrary to the Theft Act 1968. A teenage girl had used a student identity card, belonging to someone else, in order to obtain a cheaper rail fare for the midnight train to London. However, it gave me an insight of things to come.

A couple of weeks later I found myself at Bruche Police training centre, Warrington.

Thirteen weeks of total enjoyment, learning law and police skills.

Following that it was back to Liverpool, on the beat at Lime Street Station.

During my first couple of years I went on a local procedure course at the British Transport Police training school, Tadworth-on-the-Hill in Surrey, followed by a short spell in plain clothes, followed by a continuation course back at Tadworth for a month.

During this period, I had my fair share of arrests and became, what was known as, a good "thief-taker".

I had an insatiable appetite for locking up and went out each day looking for offences being committed, not as a lot of lazy bastards did, and still do, waiting for a job to be given to them, then trying their best to "cuff it".

A young recruit called Kelly was put with me. I was to mentor him as such. He asked me one day, "How do you know what to look for, you're always locking up?" My reply was simple: "From the moment you put that helmet on and walk out there, EVERYBODY IS SUSPECT. Think that way and you'll do OK." We went out on patrol and within an hour found an absconder from a Borstal. Kelly went on to make a good bobby.

My first encounter with cabin thieves was one October Sunday morning in 1974, whilst in uniform and stationed at Garston Docks, Liverpool, which was a dock that came under the British Transport Commission Ports, hence the British Transport Police, policing it, known today as Associated British Ports.

That morning I received a radio message to the effect that a German-registered ship in Stalbridge Dock had called for police assistance, as the crew had detained three males onboard.

That is when I clapped eyes on my first cabin thieves. They had been found wandering around the ship's accommodation, obviously looking for rich pickings, but this time the crew were alert.

The three of them were giving excuses of looking for work, which apparently, was a usual ploy if approached.

They were searched but, alas, nothing incriminating was found, I began questioning them, when the duty C.I.D. attended and took over.

After we searched their vehicle, which was parked on the quay side near the ship, and drew a blank, nothing incriminating was found, they were eventually warned and escorted from the dock estate.

Little did I realise then that these miscreants would come to play a major part later in my career.

Two

THE BEGINNING OF MY CID CAREER

The Beginning of my CID Career

In 1976, a new Police Force had been formed in Liverpool. It was the Port of Liverpool Police and was created primarily to carry out the policing of Liverpool Docks.

The previous policing of the docks system both on the Liverpool and Birkenhead dock estates had been carried out by Merseyside Police.

I decided to apply for a position as Detective Constable. Having looked closely at my options, I couldn't see me getting into CID where I was. It was more or less waiting for dead men's boots, unless I was prepared to move, plus having turned down the offer of a CID post at London Euston Station two years earlier.

Then there was the case of when I put a certain uniform Inspector on paper for behaving in an outrageous way and basically being a bully towards both myself and younger officers.

For his punishment, he was transferred to Bristol as a District Inspector, so I figured that I might have blotted my copybook.

Within a few days of writing, an envelope arrived, a letter asking me to attend the Port of Liverpool HQ at Canada Dock, Liverpool.

I duly attended on the given date and was ushered into an office, it looked more like a promotion board interview. I was faced with the Chief Constable, Edwin Post QPM (a lovely man, a thorough gent), Deputy Chief Constable Tom Shepherd, ex-Lancashire County and Merseyside, Detective Chief Superintendent Jim Irvine ex-City of Glasgow Police and Kent Constabulary, Superintendent Bob Physic, ex-Merseyside, and Detective Inspector John Ralphson, ex-Merseyside, who became my boss and later a very close and dear friend.

Having been grilled in the usual manner and being asked, would I not consider coming as a uniform P.C. first in order to be assessed for CID. I flatly dismissed this idea, saying it was a CID post or no post at all.

The Chief Constable thanked me for my time and told me I would be contacted in due course. Immediately I thought to myself, I've blown that one, shouldn't have been so cocky.

Having been home no more than a couple of hours the phone rang; it was Jim Irvine, the Det. Ch. Supt. informing me that the Chief Constable had decided to offer me a CID post on probation for a year.

Being a cheeky bastard, I thanked him and said I needed a day or so to think it over and make sure I was about to do the right thing. He fully understood.

I came off the phone knowing full well what my answer was and the next day wrote a letter accepting the offer.

Later that week, I tendered my resignation with British Transport Police and worked two weeks' notice, the last shift being a week of nights.

I had a week off, and then my career in CID began.

It was a Monday morning in November 1976 when I reported for duty at the Port of Liverpool Police HQ, Canada Dock, Bootle.

After meeting with Jim Irvine, the Detective Chief Superintendent, and John Ralphson, the Detective Inspector, I was taken to the CID office and there introduced to my future colleagues. There was Frank Moore, an old (well, old to me) retired Merseyside Detective, Tommy Galvin, a retired Detective Sergeant from Merseyside, Harry McCauley, retired Merseyside who was the CID admin clerk, and D.S. Tony Wrench, ex-Merseyside. Tony was the collator, with a wealth of experience in criminal intelligence. Apart from that he was quite an accomplished artist, and the walls in the admin/collator's room soon had paintings hanging from the walls, which brightened the place up. These were mainly shipping or dock related scenes, Tony had been a seaman and served on the Arctic Convoys in the war. He was always joking and had wealth of experience in the criminal intelligence sector, with contacts in lots of forces.

Jim Irvine had been headhunted by Edwin Post, the then newly appointed and first Chief Constable.

Jim, a Glaswegian by birth, had retired from Kent Constabulary and came to Liverpool to head the C.I.D. He had seen service in the SAS in North Africa during the war and joined the police after being demobbed.

He was a quiet sort; he was a serious type, but I found him extremely helpful and understanding. Sharp featured, wore spectacles, his hair was brill creamed, sort of combed back with a distinctive parting on one side. He always turned out immaculately dressed.

Just to deviate here a little, the only thing I wished at times, is that I had, had an interpreter present, as I had a job to understand his Scottish accent. I remember being called in to see him and J.R. (John Ralphson) one day to discuss a job. I nodded and agreed when I thought necessary. Afterwards J.R. jokingly said to me, "You did well in there, Paul, you only nodded once when you should have shaken your head."

Amongst my colleagues were D.C. Alex Welford, ex-Merseyside firearms unit, who mainly dealt with the shipment of explosives in and out of the port. Ken Tonge, a D.C., was the SOCO (scenes of crime officer) man, photographs and fingerprints were his forte. When he attended the scene of a burglary, there was more fingerprint powder flying around, than flour in a bakery.

D.S. Peter Heyes was an old arse Liverpool "A" Division CID officer, very well experienced, a plodder, but give him a complex matter and he seemed to thrive on it. He was a stocky chap, always wore a suit, and loved to smoke his pipe, which was like a bucket, the cunning old guy would come along to me, a fellow pipe smoker and say, "Paul can you spare me a fill", meaning he had run out of tobacco. The trouble was to fill his bucket, amounted to three of my pipe fills, that then tended to leave me having no option but to go and purchase some more tobacco, I soon learned however to buy some for him too.

Ken Candler, ex-Merseyside, had worked with the RCS (Regional Crime Squad) and was very experienced and had brilliant contacts throughout Merseyside. We seemed to gel, probably because we were both Lancashire lads. Ken had retired from Merseyside and gone working in a security role for a large company. The job didn't suit him, so he came down to the docks. I think Ken first came as a D.C. but was soon promoted to D.S. Ken was a slim, athletic type, going a little thin on top, tended to be in sports jacket and trousers more than a suit, very fit and refereed football matches, as a hobby. He also played cricket.

I owed a lot to Ken, he taught me a lot, during the time we worked together and was as keen as myself to lock up.

Later I met the Birkenhead CID officers, D.S. Fred Williams and Wilf Elliott, a D.C., both old school detectives and well experienced officers.

The reason all the Supervisory staff and C.I.D. officers were retired from other forces, was simple if you think about it, it would not have been possible to suddenly create a police force with raw recruits and inexperienced personnel. The only logical answer was recruit retiring officers from various forces, who upon their retirement were offered further employment to basically train young recruits and help the force develop. This gave those officers the opportunity of a further few years employment and an additional further small pension.

The first week was spent finding my feet, seeing how things worked and accompanying Frank Moore, who I was paired up with on enquiries, visiting the scene of thefts and burglaries.

Frank was a plodder; it was obvious he wasn't going to go the extra mile to look for an arrest but would gladly deal with a matter if need be.

When we were on a late shift, we would do any paperwork before teatime, have a scoff, usually at Marsh Lane Police Station, which was a good excuse for Frank to spend half an hour on the one-armed bandit. Then it was back to the office to hit the duty book, entering "Called Passing", then usually to Fairfield Police club for several pints and more arm exercise on the bandit there.

I would ring in a couple of times to see if there were any incidents that required our attendance, which of course might interrupt Frank's activities.

I recall spoiling his plans one evening. We were going out the front door of the station towards where the CID cars were parked. Out of the corner of my eye, in the shadows I saw a figure about to leave the dock estate via a hole in the dock perimeter fence. I went over, and it was a docker who came from the direction of the T.J. Harrison berth in Canada Dock. I stopped him and carried out a quick body search. Bingo, there was a bottle of whisky concealed in his inside pocket. As I told him I was arresting him, I could read Frank's face. The expression more or less said, "Shit, there goes my pint."

Frank did teach me a lot. He was a nice guy, but I felt I was being restricted. So, having found my feet after six months or so, myself and Ken Candler tended to work together more. We secured some good convictions.

At this time, we were experiencing reports of thefts of cash from Captains' cabins, on a weekly basis, in fact they were increasing by the month. Tony Wrench had started to collate info about known and suspected cabin thieves who were operating. All these suspects were from the Bootle area of Merseyside.

He collected a lot of intelligence from Merseyside Police and the Manchester Docks Police, who not only covered Manchester Docks (what was left of it) but the ports along the Manchester Ship Canal, such as Irlam, Partington, Runcorn and as far as Ellesmere Port. The intelligence was entered into the card index file in his office (there were no computers then), so it was a detailed job, cross-referencing each individual and, separately, the cars they were known to be using, together with known associates.

One day in early 1977, Ken and myself stopped a car in Huskisson dock avenue. on Liverpool Docks. Onboard were three of our suspects and, funny enough, I recognised two of the three as being the same suspects I had dealt with at Garston Docks a few years earlier.

We decided to take more of an interest in this group and collated as much info as possible on them, soon discovering that the team was quite extended, approximately twenty-plus in all. Any information or sighting Ken and I gathered was passed onto Tony Wrench.

The main players (seven in all) tended to operate in teams of two or three, but sometimes you would get one of the others in there.

Tony had gathered intelligence which showed the cabin thieves were visiting other ports: throughout the U.K. Manchester Docks, Hull, Goole, Grimsby, Scunthorpe, Ellesmere Port, Preston, Dundee, Avonmouth, the south Wales docks of Swansea, Cardiff and Newport, Tilbury and others.

Details of theft and sightings were coming in thick and fast. They really had spread their wings and obviously found easy pickings.

THE M.O. (MODUS OPERANDI)

During the first six months of 1977 numerous offences of thefts of sterling and foreign currencies were reported by the masters of vessels berthed in Liverpool. The modus operandi used by the offenders was to operate in interchanging teams of two, three or four, select a foreign vessel, usually Greek, Spanish or Mediterranean based vessels as their target, sneak into the captains' quarters and steal cash from safe therein.

It is appropriate to mention at this point considerable sums of differing currencies are accrued by the captains from various ports, for the purpose of victualling or paying wages. Those monies, quite often amounting to equivalent totals of over £10,000 Sterling were sometimes kept in drawers, or in safes, the keys to which were kept in open drawers, and in the instances of safes provided with combination locking devices, the combination was written on a piece of paper and kept available in a drawer There were also instances where forcible entry had been made into the cabins, either through the door or a port-hole.

In the unlikely event of the suspects being challenged whilst on board a vessel, they purported to be ships chandlers, freshwater men, seamen seeking employment or seeking an acquaintance who they believed was part of the crew. For the most part those frivolous reasons for being on the vessel were accepted, and they remained free to roam the vessel at will.

Most ships captains carried a float of cash in their safe, anything from a few hundred pounds to twenty thousand-plus. If, say, a Greek ship left Piraeus, the captain probably had a couple of thousands of pounds worth of Greek drachma (no euro then) in the safe so he could pay his crew on arrival at the next port. After all, the crew wanted a few beers ashore and to get their leg over with the ladies of the night. Prior to arrival at the next port, the captain would send a message contacting the local ship's agent there and order sufficient stock to victual the ship. But to be able to pay for these goods, he had the ship's agent at the port bring him cash onboard, or in the UK a security company would carry out this task. So, if he was arriving in Naples, he would be given Italian lira, or in a French port, French francs. After he had paid the invoice and crew, he had cash left over again. This could be the equivalent of a thousand pounds or more. Therefore, on his six-month trip before docking at, say, Liverpool (where the same procedure took place), he probably had anything from £3,000 to £15,000 of mixed currency lying in his safe, sometimes even far larger amounts.

Now, wait for it, where did the captain keep his key to the safe when he left his cabin at mealtimes to join his fellow officers in the dining salon: in his possession? No, it was either in the top desk drawer or under a potted plant on top of the safe, and furthermore his cabin door was left open or unlocked. As I say, the whole situation led to easy pickings for a very smart bunch of thieves.

Three

THE EARLY YEARS

The Early Years

In the spring of 1977, I went on a Home Office residential CID course at the Merseyside Police Training School, Mather Avenue, Liverpool.

On the Friday prior to my course, there was a bottle on in the CID office, as was the norm in those days. It would be opened around 4.30 p.m. and Tony Wrench would ring around the offices to announce, "The starlings have landed." That was the code that a bottle of Scotch was about to be cracked. This, of course, wasn't just limited to Fridays.

On this particular occasion John Ralphson presented me with a good-quality pen in a presentation box for my course.

By now you are probably wondering how the phrase "the starlings have landed" came about. Well, one Monday afternoon around 4.30 p.m. John Ralphson, the D.I., had produced a bottle in Tony Wrench's office. It was a November afternoon, and I hadn't been there more than a week. As they were pouring out a few wee drams, starlings were seen to be massing and landing on a dock warehouse, going to roost for the night, hence the phrase "THE STARLINGS HAVE LANDED." I always remember J. R, being a Royalist like myself, used to put a bottle on, when it was the Queen's birthday (both official and other). On one occasion, he toasted the Queen, raising his glass and saying,

"HER MAJESTY", in a low voice Mick Hughes added "and the Corgis". Everyone laughed.

I spent ten weeks on the CID course, which I enjoyed immensely. We worked hard and played hard, and I made quite a few friends from other forces. I teamed up with a lad from my old force, the British Transport Police, called Wayne Clayton, we became good friends.

Upon my return, it was a case of getting back into the routine.

In June that year, two more officers joined the CID department, Ron Peace and Mike Hughes, both coming over from the Ministry of Defence Police. Around that time, I can't quite recall when, but others came onboard too. There was Les Evans, Jock Meek and Jack Holt, all retired Merseyside officers. Mike Hughes and I worked together quite a lot, and we had some good arrests. Mike, however, leant more towards drug-related enquiries whereas I stayed focused on cabin thieves. This, of course, was apart from our day-to-day investigation work. Eventually Mike was posted to Birkenhead, so I didn't see much of him after that.

Now, I am digressing a little here by adding the following, which I think will be of interest to those readers who are not familiar with what is involved, behind the scenes, when policing a Royal visit.

ROYAL VISIT

That year, 1977, was the Queen's Silver Jubilee, and Her Majesty visited Liverpool amongst other towns and cities throughout the UK.

When Her Majesty visited Liverpool, not only did she tour the city but she reviewed a fleet of Royal Navy ships and merchant vessels anchored in the river Mersey, she inspected them by sailing up and down the river on a Mersey ferry, the aptly named *Royal Iris*. I found myself being attached to the Merseyside Police special branch for the day, as liaison officer and assisting in close protection duties, accompanying the Royal party onboard the ferry.

On the morning of 21st June 1977, I signed on duty at 5 a.m. at Police HQ Canada Dock, after collecting what I needed. I was driven to the berth where the *Royal Iris* was moored. It was a beautiful summer's morning, the sun shining and warming up nicely. As I boarded the ferry, a team of Navy divers were emerging from beneath, having checked the hull for any limpet mines, etc. The Detective Inspector in charge made himself known to me, then introduced me to a Detective Sergeant and two more officers. We were all very smartly dressed in our best suits for the occasion. There was a team of painters and decorators onboard. Carpenters had removed all the side plywood panels, which ran along the sides of the deck walkway, in order that a thorough search could be carried out by a Customs Rummage crew for explosive devices (this was in the midst of IRA troubles in the 1970s). Once it was deemed safe, and was clear of any explosive devises, the panels were replaced and the painters gave the panels a fresh coat of paint, which by 10 a.m. was as dry as a bone. You couldn't tell a painting job had been done.

We sailed up and down the river to pass the time away, finally berthing at Seacombe ferry landing stage, Birkenhead, at around noon, where some beautiful potted plants were brought onboard for decorative purposes. My job was to scan these with a machine for explosive devices.

Then off we went again up and down the river. It was very nice, I must say, rather pleasant. We just needed a few beers and a buffet, and the job would have been perfect.

Just prior to 3 p.m. we entered Langton Dock, various dignitaries boarded, and shortly afterwards the Royal Party arrived by car. I was stood at the bottom of the gangway on the ferry with one of the Special Branch officers on the other side opposite me. Her Majesty and Prince Philip came down the gangway onto the ferry with the Lord Lieutenant Sir Douglas Crawford, who upon seeing me smiled. He used to shoot on an estate where I went beating and picking up in those days.

The Royal Party were seated on a small, raised stage on the aft deck, a wooden structure surrounded on three sides with bulletproof glass. One of us stood either side. The review was carried out, the ferry sailing up and down the river going in and out of the fleet of anchored ships, eventually returning to the Pier Head landing stage in Liverpool, where the Queen and party alighted and walked a very short distance to the Royal Yacht *Britannia* berthed close by. That was it, my day over, home for a few well-earned pints in my local hostelry.

This was not the first time I had carried out Royal duties. (Again, I'm including the following account for the benefit of the less experienced amongst you. I think you will be surprised by it). Whilst in uniform with my old force the British Transport Police, I was rostered together with a Sergeant Ozzy Porteous and five other officers to spend the night at Lowton railway sidings, near Warrington, guarding the Royal train. Lowton is an isolated railway siding just off the main line, easily accessible by car, right next to a country lane road bridge. The only nearby building was a public house which stood at the foot of the bridge (now remember that it's very important).

We took up duties at around 7 p.m. that evening and used a plate-layer's hut in the sidings as our base. It was OK. We could make a brew, as there was a stove of sorts which had been left lit for us and also provided some heat. Although it was summertime it did get cooler in the early hours.

We made a thorough search of the sidings, obviously for security reasons.

Shortly afterwards, the Royal train entered the sidings, and the engine unhooked and left. The coaches consisted of three, the Royal party's coach, the servants' coach, and the Police Protection team coach at the rear. Ozzy took three of us out to meet the train, detailing one officer to stand at each end of the carriages and one to patrol continually around the train. We did one-hour stints before being relieved by the other officers. Meanwhile, Ozzy had settled himself down in the hut on a bench for forty winks, Hmm!

Come 4.30 a.m. the next day, it was a lovely morning the sun was breaking through, and a slight mist was rising. I was stood at the front coach and could see two very smartly dressed men, suited and booted, wearing bowler hats and pin striped three-piece suits. One was carrying a clip board and the other a "wheel-tapper's hammer". They were British Rail Managers.

I stopped them and checked their authority, they would already, have had to pass an initial police checkpoint, as there were about thirty officers from the local force positioned in the fields all around and further down the line. Once I had cleared them, the chap with the hammer tapped every wheel on all the carriages, listening for odd noises which would indicate any cracks or faults. The other guy ticked his sheet after each wheel had been checked. Once that procedure was completed, they returned in the direction from whence they came.

About thirty minutes later came two more guys, dressed the same, one carrying a small wooden ladder, which I suppose was about a yard or so high and came to a point at the top. Again, I checked them out, then allowed them to carry on. The guy with the ladder put it up against each carriage door, breathed hard on the already shining brass handles, then polished the handle with a yellow duster, his colleague of course ticking his paperwork as they went around. Once all handles were duly polished, they left. After about half an hour, an engine entered the sidings, coupled up to the carriages, and the Royal train left. By this time, it was about 6 a.m. We then walked to the nearby pub joining the other officers, about thirty-five of us in all sat down for a fully cooked breakfast, washed down with a couple of pints of beer. You could have had tea or coffee, I suppose. All paid for by the job.

So, after reading this account and the previous, I hope this gives you (the inexperienced) a better understanding of just what goes on behind the scenes when a Royal visit takes place. I doubt now, though, that the informal breakfast and a couple of pints whilst on duty would be looked on favourably, in this politically correct, snowflake society in which we live.

On 16th May 1978, our Detective Chief Supt., Jim Irvine, hosted a crime conference. Officers from various Port Police Forces and local forces attended, together with representatives from the Central Drugs and Illegal Immigration Unit, New Scotland Yard.

The problems of drug importation and cabin thieves were the main topics discussed.

It was then that Jim announced that the collation of intelligence in relation to the cabin thieves would (providing everyone agreed) be co-ordinated by the Port of Liverpool Police and was to be given the operational name of "CABINET", so Operation Cabinet was born (meaning "net" the cabin thieves).

The sole idea at this point in time was to accumulate and distribute intelligence to all interested parties, the idea of a full-blown operation, with prosecutions, had not been considered.

This conference led to a much closer co-operation between forces, especially the British Transport Police of the Humber ports division and us. By then our cabin thieves were hitting ships in the Humber estuary, at Hull, Immingham, Goole, and Grimsby on a regular basis. From what we were told, by Merseyside Police officers who had dealt with the problem of thefts from ships cabins before we came into existence. Our suspects had progressed from being young teenagers, visiting ships selling newspapers to crew, spotting an opportunity to steal, when they came across an unoccupied cabin and finding monies lying around. To becoming a more experienced, professional Burglar by the age of Twenty and of course having their own transport, meant they could then visit various ports throughout the U.K.

As a result of that closeness we learned that the Dutch Ports of Rotterdam and Amsterdam, together with Antwerp in Belgium, were also being hit hard, so we now had an international gang on our hands.

Over the next couple of years, we continued to stop and search suspects as they came to notice in and around the docks, but seldom had we sufficient evidence to prosecute for specific offences, and thefts were still occurring, undetected.

Our predecessors, Merseyside Police, had also encountered the same problems as we were having: either nothing incriminating was found on the suspects or, if there was sufficient evidence, they would plead not guilty knowing it would be near impossible to fly the witnesses back to the UK to give evidence in a court case. This meant the suspects were off the hook with no further action being taken. The team were very good at avoiding their presence being detected whilst inside the dock estates, they would visit at peak times, between noon and 2 p.m. and 5 p.m. to 6 p.m., times when dockers were coming and going for meal breaks in large numbers and ships' crews gathering in the galley for their meal. They blended in and were seldom spotted.

One day in early 1979, myself and another officer attended a report of a theft of money from a Greek ship. The captain was reporting the theft of a large amount of cash approx. £7000 from his safe. It transpired he had left his safe key in a desk drawer, leaving his cabin unlocked whilst he went to the officers dining room for lunch. Upon his return to his cabin, he found the safe unlocked and the cash missing.

When I sat down with him to take details, he burst into tears, it transpired that, as it would be deemed by his bosses to be his fault, leaving the cabin door unlocked, he would be held liable for the money and would have to work for the best part of a year to repay the debt. He was a married man with a young family.

This incident struck home with me and I thought something had to be done to curtail the activities of these thieving bastards, not only were they committing thefts, but they were ruining people's lives.

On numerous occasions were had carried out observations, near to a ship that we thought may be an appetising target for our suspects, to hit, but to no avail. I had borrowed vans and other vehicles, so as not to stand out, we even sat on warehouse roofs with binoculars, again we drew a blank. I recall Ken Candler telling me one day when we were discussing something else, about Lenny Gowing, a Detective Sergeant on the Crime squad, who apparently had a saying, "Softly, softly, catch a monkey". With that in mind, I thought not only are we spending countless hours on observations, even if we did get lucky and managed to arrest a couple of our suspects, the same old problem would likely occur, the ship sails, no witnesses, case dismissed. Furthermore, we would only have maybe Two or Three suspects, so I started to think more on the lines of a conspiracy charge against our suspects with a softly, softly approach.

That year I began to create a file on each of the suspects, extracting information from the files Tony Wrench had collated and from intelligence Ken and I had gathered. This was added to constantly. Each file comprised of personal details, a mug shot, any significant marks to the body such as tattoos etc, that had been noted previously, list of convictions etc. Each file also listed, dates times and places of incidents they could be linked to, arrests, stop checks, vehicles etc and known associates, quite comprehensive really.

It was at this time that we created warning posters, in various languages, which we handed out to ships' officers and lock-gate men for distribution to visiting vessels arriving in port (see Figure 2).

During this period of part-time work on Cabinet, some other interesting occurrences took place, and I have included this little story which still makes me smile to this day.

We had a Deputy Chief Constable, Tom Shepherd, who was an ex-Lancashire and Merseyside man. He was an ex-Fleet Air Arm, officer, and it showed. Everyone was addressed by their surname.

Figure 2: Warning Poster

WARNING

THERE MAY BE A THIEF ABOUT.
KEEP YOUR CABIN LOCKED.
SECURE YOUR VALUABLES.
DO NOT ALLOW STRANGERS
ABOARD YOUR SHIP
WITHOUT AUTHORITY.

REPORT ANY SUSPICIOUS
INCIDENT IMMEDIATELY
TO PORT POLICE
TEL. 933 8393

WARNUNG

ES BESTEHT DIE MOEG-LICHKEIT, daß
einige Diebe an Bord Kommen. BEVOR
Sie IHRE CABINE verlassen, überzeugen
Sie sich davon dass alle Fenster
Geschlossen sind. ALLETUEREN
Schließen. ERLAUBEN SIE KEINEM
UMBEKANNTEN DAS SCHIFF
zu betreten.

MELDEN SIE BITTE GEDEN
DIEBSTAHL oder jede Ungewöhnlichkeit
der Hafen Polizei.
TEL No. 933 8393

WAARSCHUWING

SLUIT UW HUT AF WANT
ER KOMEN HIER NOG WEL
EENS DIEVEN.
WAARDEVOLLE ARTIKELEN
ACHTER SLOT EN GRENDEL
LAAT GEEN VREEMDEN AAN
BOORD ZONDER TOESTEMMING

RAPPORTEER · VERDACHTE
VOORVALLEN ONMIDDELYK
AAN DE HAVEN POLITIE.
TEL. No. 933 8393

ADVARSEL

Der er muligvis en tyv om bord.
Hold Deres dør lukket og låst.
Lås Deres værdier inde.
Tillad ingen fremmede om bord uden
autorisation.

Rapporter alle mistænkeligheder
øjeblikkelig til:
Port Police
Tlf. No. 933 8393

ADVERTENCIA

POR POSIBILIDADES DE ROBO:
MANTENGA SUS CABINAS
CERRADAS ASEGURE SUS
VALORES NO PERMITA EXTRAÑOS
A BORDO DE LA NAUE.
SIN ANTORIZACION DE LAS
AUTORIDADES.

INFORME CUALQUIER SUPUESTO
INCIDENTE INMEDIATAMENTE
A LA POLICIA DEL PUERTO
TELEFONO No. 933 8393

ΠΡΟΕΙΔΟΠΟΙΗΣΙΣ

ΠΥΘΑΝΩΝ ΕΔΩ ΝΑ ΠΕΡΙΦΕΡΕΤΑΙ
ΕΝΑΣ ΚΛΕΦΤΗΣ
ΚΡΑΤΑΤΕ ΤΗΣ ΚΑΜΠΙΝΕΣ ΣΑΣ ΚΛΕΙΣΤΕΣ
ΑΣΦΑΛΙΣΕΤΑΙ ΤΑ ΠΟΛΥΤΙΜΑ
ΣΑΣΑΝΤΙΚΕΙΜΕΝΑ ΜΗΝ ΕΠΙΤΡΕΠΕΤΑΙ
ΞΕΝΟΥΣ ΕΠΙ ΤΟΥ ΠΛΟΙΟΥ ΕΑΝ ΔΕΝ
ΕΙΝΑΙ ΕΞΟΥΣΙΟΔΟ ΑΝΑΦΕΡΑΤΕ ΚΑΘΕ

ΥΠΟΠΤΟ ΣΥΜΒΑΝ ΣΤΗΝ ΛΙΜΕΝΙΚΗ
ΑΣΤΥΝΟΜΙΑ ΑΜΕΣΩΣ
ΤΗΜΕΝΟΙ ΤΗΛ/ΝΟ 9338393

One winter's evening, whilst driving the Red CID car, I had a slight mishap and damaged the sump. Taffy Bates, the uniform sergeant, who was salt of the earth, said I had better give him a report covering the incident, which I did. Outlining the incident, describing how I had seen the figure of a man dodging in and out of the shadows (not the black dog, as most County Force officers would have included, not many dogs loose on the docks) as I drove along next to the railway lines in Huskisson Dock. Failing to notice a signal point lever sticking up, which I drove over, and it damaged the sump on the car.

Two days later, when returning to duty, I was summoned to Shepherd's office. He told me he was grounding me for three months. In other words, I was not allowed to drive police vehicles, so someone had to chauffer me around for that period of time.

Sure, enough three months later, on a beautiful sunny Monday morning, whilst sat at my desk typing up crime reports the office phone rang. Shepherd wanted to see me. I put my jacket on and went along the corridor to his office.

I can remember his exact words: "I'm giving you your wings back young man, be careful in the future."

I returned to my typing. It was about 9.45 a.m. and Ken Candler was about to leave for court. He drew my attention, pointing to a van through the office window which we could see parked inside the West Canada Dock warehouse. We were aware that there was a Brazilian ship berthed nearby, which was unloading a shipment of corned beef.

Grabbing a set of car keys with Mick Hughes accompanying me, I drove around to the dock avenue leading to the warehouse. As we did so, the suspect van, which was a Thames trader type, was heading towards us in the distance. With the police sign up in the window, I began flashing my lights for the driver to stop. The van was clearly laden, the arse end was nearly touching the floor. As we neared each other, he would go to his right and I to my left. Clearly, he wasn't going to stop. As we were yards apart, I told Mick to brace himself and we collided, I really have no idea how that could have happened! There was the usual crunching sound, experienced in an accident, my front driver's wing crumpled, and the bonnet buckled. We came to a sudden halt. Mick, as quick as a flash, leapt from our car and went to the driver, who was struggling in an attempt to slide his door open, I heard him say, "Laurence, you're nicked." (We knew the offender from a previous encounter.) I couldn't open the driver's door. It had jammed with the impact. The passenger door on the van was apparently also knackered, preventing any escape. After radioing for assistance and the prisoner and Mick being taken away, myself and the CID car were towed back to Police HQ.

As we passed the front door of the nick, I saw Shepherd stood with Jim Irvine. He looked at the CID car with me behind the wheel, slapped his flat hand onto his forehead and blurted out something out. I later discovered at was a line from `Victor Meldrew`, with an added word. "I don't fucking believe it".

When the van was examined, it was found to be fully laden with cartons of corned beef.

We charged the client with the Burglary/ theft of £4,000 worth of corned beef. He was duly dealt with at court later.

Funny enough I didn't get grounded again!

Now, the CID car in question was the same car I had previously had the mishap in, so there is a moral to this story: don't drive Red C.I.D cars, they're unlucky.

Between August 1979 and January 1980 our suspects were highly active, as you will see from a specimen few instances I have listed here:

> *18th August 1979. Three suspects stopped in suspicious circumstances at Goole Docks.*
>
> At 12.30pm that day an HGV driver working at Goole docks noticed a Green Triumph 2000 saloon car with Three men on board enter the docks at speed, after coming to a halt near the M.V. `ALAMA which was berthed there. The driver noticed two of the occupants were walking towards the ship, the car driver staying behind the wheel. They were approached and **Suspect P** gave an excuse of looking for a friend who he thought was on board. (The driver who was later identified from photographs as a person not in our main list of suspects but does figure in chapter Three, in The Canadian Job and was the person sentenced.) The witness became suspicious and went to seek police assistance. The team obviously panicked and left the docks. British Transport police began a search of the area and notified the local force giving a description of the car and its occupants. The vehicle was eventually located and stopped nearby,

the three occupants were questioned and searched, there was a copy of the Journal of Commerce newspaper in the car, daily shipping lists were published in that paper, giving ships names, nationalities and arrival dates at U.K. ports. Obviously, our team had used this as a reference to newly arriving vessels, which would be prime targets. The other occupant in the car was a person who later became one of our main suspects.

All three were released and warned not to visit the dock estate again.

12th September 1979. Two suspects detained at Tranmere oil terminal, Birkenhead.

At around 1pm that day the wife of the second mate, who was staying on board the vessel` the M.V. SERENIA` berthed there, came across three men walking around the ship, they were seen to enter the aft accommodation and were acting suspiciously. She returned to her cabin and ensured it was locked, then went to the ships office to inform someone of what she had just seen. On her way to the office she came across one of the men stood outside the Captain's cabin. The Chief Officer was made aware and a search of the ship was made. The Chief Officer located the three men in the lounge near to the Captains quarters. They were approached and gave excuses of looking for work. After being told there were no jobs going and before being asked to leave, they asked if they could have a sandwich (cheeky bastards) the officer told them to help themselves. A short time later the officer returned to the galley and upon not being able to locate the men, organised a search of the ship.

The police were summoned, and the suspects located, they were identified as **Suspect P and** the two suspects mentioned in the previous incident in Goole. All three were interviewed and released with a warning not to visit the dock estate.

17th September 1979. Two suspects warned for being on Liverpool dock estate.

At around 11.45am that day D.C. Matty Maxwell and myself were driving along Regent Road, Bootle, (The dock Road, which runs alongside the dock estate for several miles) when we saw a known suspects' car being driven South along that road. We turned around and saw the vehicle being parked in Brunswick Place, near to Canada Dock. Two of our suspects alighted from the vehicle, crossed the road, and entered the docks. They were seen to walk along the quayside, looking at ships berthed there and then leave via the same dock gate. We approached them asking why they had been into the dock estate. Both gave excuses of looking for a mate. Both were warned to stay off the dock estate and allowed to leave.

17th October 1979 Three suspects stopped and warned.

At 2.55pm that day, Constable McCabe was on duty at Langton street dock gate, Liverpool Docks, when he saw one of our known suspects vehicles entering the dock estate. He caused the vehicle to stop and saw it was occupied by three of our known suspects. They were questioned and gave an excuse of looking for work. They were warned not to visit the dock estate and left.

24th October 1979. One suspect found in Liverpool dock estate and warned.

At 9.10pm that day, two officers were on mobile patrol within the Liverpool Dock estate and near to Gladstone Dock when they noticed another one of our suspects vehicles parked near to the M.V. `Aldgate` berthed there. Observations were kept and at 9.50pm one of our suspects was seen to return to the vehicle, he had not been seen to visit or leave the vessel. He drove away to leave the dock estate. The officers radioed ahead, and the vehicle was stopped at Crosby Road Dock gate. The occupant was searched nothing incriminating was found on him or in the vehicle, he refused to give a reason for being on the dock estate and was allowed to go after being warned not to visit the dock estate.

Sunday 11th November 1979. Three suspects were detained by crew members on Korean ship in Birkenhead Docks, warned and seen from the dock estate.

At around 17.40hrs that afternoon the Captain of the M.V. World Virtue berthed at the Liverpool Grain Storage, Dock Road, Birkenhead called for police assistance after having found three men wandering around his vessel. Port Police officers attended and discovered the crew had detained **Suspect**, **P**, **D** and **T**, from our list of suspects. From enquiries made it appeared the Captain had been disturbed by a male person the previous day whilst resting in his cabin. However, that person was not one of the three detained. The suspects were searched, questioned, and allowed to go as nothing incriminating was found, and they gave excuses of looking for work.

19th November 1979. Two suspects were detained on Ellesmere Port Docks and warned.

In the evening, two officers of the Manchester Dock police who were on duty at Ellesmere port docks came across a known suspects' car, parked alongside a Greek vessel berthed there the M.V. `ARKANDROS`. The time was 9.20pm. The officers boarded the vessel and made a search but could not locate the driver. They returned to the dock gate entrance and waited, after a short time the vehicle attempted to leave the dock estate, it was stopped, the driver was **Suspect D**, who when questioned stated he had given a lift to a seaman he met, who wanted to return to his ship. Both he and the vehicle were searched with negative result, he was warned as to his presence on the dock estate and allowed to go.

Wednesday 16th January 1980. Avonmouth Docks, Bristol.

On this occasion the M.V. `ALBRIGHT PIONEER` was berthed at Avonmouth Docks. At 16.30hrs that afternoon the Captain was returning to his cabin along a corridor, his attention was drawn to a closed door near to his cabin, that door lead to the bonded locker. He opened the door and found three men attempting to open a door that gave access to the boat deck. After questioning them and having been given futile explanations, he saw them from the ship. He then rang the police and reported the matter. He noted all three had Liverpudlian accents. The police attended and took details of the incident, noting the car registration number, the men were seen to leave in, the captain had noted this.

Avon and Somerset police were informed and a short while later the vehicle in question was stopped by the police on the M5 motorway. The suspects and vehicle were searched, nothing incriminating was found.

On the morning of Wednesday 23rd January 1980, a vehicle known to be used by our suspects was seen on the Birkenhead dock estate by two police officers.

The vehicle was parked near to Duke street. The officers approached it and found two of our **Suspects, B** and **D**, sat in the vehicle. The occupants were questioned and gave an excuse of visiting a nearby scrap yard for a vehicle part. They were warned as to their presence on the dock estate and allowed to go.

The problem at Birkenhead Dock estate was that it was an open dock estate with roads running through it. There was no perimeter fencing or gates that were Police controlled.

26th January 1980. Theft of 1,000 US dollars, suspect detained, one ran away, no further action, no monies recovered.

On this occasion The M.V. `JUANITA HALKIAS` was berthed at East Mortar Mill Quay, Birkenhead Docks. The Captain was sat in the smoke room on board, the time was around 7.40am. He saw two men walking around the ship. Hearing a noise, he went to investigate and saw some crew members had detained one of the men. It transpired a theft of monies had taken place from a cabin, the suspects had been disturbed and tried to escape. The second suspect made it to the quay side, upon seeing his accomplice was detained he produced the money and offered it back to the crew, asking them to release his friend. He then changed his mind and ran away. It was discovered 1000 U.S. Dollars had been stolen from an officer's cabin.

The police attended, **Suspect T,** was arrested and later charged with the Burglary/Theft of the money. The other offender was never traced, and no money was recovered. The ship sailed, the witnesses with it and the matter was not pursued through the courts.

On Wednesday 30th January 1980, the M.V. `THORHAMER` was berthed in Trafford Wharf, Manchester Docks.

At around 12noon the Captain left his cabin but before doing so placed his wallet in his desk drawer. It contained £80 Sterling and 50 Deutsche Marks. He left his cabin door open and went to the see a crew member. Upon his return a short time later, he saw a man stood on the bridge deck above where his cabin was located. The man asked him if there was any work, after the

Captain informed him there was none, this person left the ship and walked away.

The Captain returned to his cabin and then discovered the money had been taken from his wallet. Another officer had also encountered the male person on board, who was asking for a job. Detectives John Morris and Billy Daws of the Manchester dock police were parked nearby in an observation van. They saw the male leave the ship and get into a vehicle which was known to be used by our suspects. As the vehicle attempted to leave the dock estate, it was stopped. The passenger ran off making good his escape. The driver **Suspect K** was detained whilst enquiries were made on board. The suspect was then interviewed by Detective Sergeant John Hannon and later bailed to appear at a later date whilst further enquiries were made. No further action was taken against the suspect in this matter and the person who ran off was never traced.

The above list of incidents I hope gives you, the reader, a flavour of events as they occurred, in that short period of time.

In all the above incidents bar Two, there was no theft of monies, just suspects found in suspicious circumstances and warned to stay off the dock estates. In between these incidents taking place, thefts of currency had been occurring at various ports throughout the UK, but no suspects were sighted or identified, and no doubt visits had been made to various ports, which were undetected.

In June 1980 two of our suspects were arrested in Rotterdam and were found to be in possession of false British Visitor Passports. The Dutch police contacted our office, and we were able to identify the pair by their tattoos, from the personal files previously prepared. It then became apparent that far more liaison was needed between forces, especially with those on the continent.

HAVE WHEELS WILL TRAVEL

On Wednesday 20th August 1980, the Greek Vessel M.V. Zarathrusta was berthed at King George Wharf, Dundee Docks, Scotland. She was unloading a cargo of Jute.

At 8.30 p.m. that evening the Captain left his cabin to attend to other matters on board. At 9.30 p.m. whilst he was sat in another part of the ship, the Captain saw two men walk past a port hole window on the outer deck. He rushed out and challenged them, noticing one of the males had an identifying mark on his neck. They gave a plausible explanation as to their presence on board and were allowed to leave. At 10.30 p.m. he returned to his cabin and found the port hole window open, showing signs of forcible entry, he checked his safe but was unable to open it. It had not only been relocked, but the combination lock had been spun (activated) and as he never used the combination he couldn't remember or locate the code, so he was unable to open it. The safe had contained £500 Sterling, 1600 US Dollars, 4000 Belgian Francs, and a quantity of Deutsch Marks and some Egyptian Pounds, totalling around £1450 Sterling. Also, ampules of Morphine and a .38 Pistol and ammunition. A security guard was present when the Captain spoke to the two men and noticed their strong Liverpudlian accents.

A locksmith was employed by the Police and opened the safe, it was then confirmed the contents were missing.

The then Tayside Police force, referred to our entry in the Scottish Police Gazette and managed to identify one of our suspects from a photograph and a detailed description.

The suspects details were immediately circulated, and it was known the identified suspect frequented Ilfracombe in Devon, so both Merseyside Police, We and the Devon and Cornwall Police were made aware of the incident.

Lo and behold at 11.33 p.m. the following day, Thursday 21st August, an astute Sergeant in Ilfracombe spotted the suspect, who was known to him, about to enter a night club there. He duly arrested him.

The suspect was later transported to Dundee for questioning. He was charged with the offence but later no action was taken due to the ship and witnesses having left Port. Again, the suspects had avoided prosecution.

So, our suspect had driven over 250 miles from Liverpool to Dundee to commit the theft, then driven down to Devon a further 500 miles, all in two days.

IF YOU CANNOT GAIN ENTRY TO A SAFE, WHY NOT TAKE THE WHOLE THING AWAY

Well I suppose if you can't get into a safe, the logical answer is to take the safe and this is what happened next.

On Wednesday 10th September 1980, the M.V. Esperanza was berthed at Immingham Docks on the Humber estuary.

At 6 p.m. that evening the Captain returned to his cabin and went to the cupboard which should have contained the ship's safe, containing £2500 in Bank of England notes, 30,000 Greek Drachma, one .32 pistol and 50 rounds of ammunition, together with ampules of Morphine and other medication was missing. Yes, as the offender obviously couldn't open the safe and as it wasn't too heavy, he nicked it.

Enquiries on board showed a seaman had come across two English men on board the ship at around 5 p.m. He noticed them leaving the ship and one was carrying something heavy wrapped in brown paper and placing it on the back seat of a car park on the quayside.

Further enquiries by British Transport Police lead them to believe the offender seen by the seaman was one of our suspects.

On Monday 15th September D.I. Cliff Hardcastle and D.C. Rod Bradley came over to Liverpool bringing the Greek witnesses with them. We visited a pub in Bootle where, we knew the suspects frequented. I, Cliff, and Rod went inside, as we did, we saw a group of our suspects seated in another room. It was at this point our prime suspect was identified by the witness and he began to leave the pub. Cliff Hardcastle challenged him, he ran into a nearby street, I was a little fitter in those days, gave chase and detained him.

He was arrested and taken back to Grimsby for questioning. He was charged with the offence, however as had become the norm in these cases, the ship sailed, so did our witnesses and the charge, was not pursued. Again, the offender walked away Scott free.

Following the above arrest, Detective Inspector Cliff Hardcastle of the British Transport Police, Humber Ports Division, contacted our office and sought assistance in mounting a series of raids on several known suspects house, whom he thought may have been involved in the above offence. It was hoped that some piece of evidence would be found, to link into the Immingham offence or at least we would find something that linked to other offences that had been committed.

He discussed the matter with J.R. and `Operation Greek` was set for a series of raids to be carried out the following morning, 25th September 1980.

J.R. had sought the assistance of Detective Chief Inspector McMasters of the Regional Crime squad as a total of Seven addresses were going to be searched. Very early on the morning of Thursday 25th September 1980, Cliff arrived at our H.Q. with a team of Seven of his men, we had a team of Six officers which included myself and Ken Candler and there were a number of R.C.S. officers to assist.

All the target houses were `hit` simultaneously at 7am and searched, unfortunately nothing was found to link any other suspects with the Immingham offence

THE M.V. GIANNIS. N. INCIDENT- LIVERPOOL DOCKS

On Wednesday 19th November 1980, the M.V. Giannis. N. was berthed at the Grain terminal, Seaforth Docks, Liverpool. She was discharging a cargo of loose grain.

At around 5.45pm that evening, the Captain was sitting in his office on board, preparing to pay the crew their wages, after having received a considerable amount of currency in Bank of England notes, which had been brought on board earlier that day, by a security company. He heard the Chief Mate shouting" Captain, Captain" several times. Upon looking out of the cabin door, he saw the Chief Mate had hold of a male person and was coming down the steps which led to the bridge. This person was later identified as our **Suspect L.** The captain kept hold of the suspect whilst his fellow officer rang for police assistance. Some crew members were put on alert and began to search and watch the ships corridors.

When the chief mate returned to the captain, he took some crew with him and then went to search the bridge area. There they found another male person hiding, he was identified as out **Suspect P.** He was brought down the stairway to join the other suspect. At this point a violent struggle took place,

The chief officer chased a third man, but he managed to flee the ship and was being chased by some men, who turned out to be myself and other officers, along the quayside.

It was at this point that Mick Hughes, me and another officer went to the ship after receiving a radio message, informing us of the circumstances. As we neared the gangway, Mick who was driving brought the car to a halt and I saw one of our suspects who we recognised as, **Suspect D,** run from the ship, we all gave chase. Mick and our other colleague chased after him, following him into a dock shed. I ran to the other end of the shed to cut off any means of escape. Ken Candler then joined us; he had also been alerted by radio. After a short time, Mick and Jock Meek brought our suspect out of the dock shed, they had found him hiding on a conveyor belt. He looked like a snow man, covered in dust as a result of grain being constantly moved by the conveyor belt system.

Together with Ken Candler I boarded the ship and met up with the officers and the captain and our two other suspects. There was a violent struggle taking place and lots of shouting. After briefly ascertaining the facts, I arrested **Suspect P**, and began to lead him down the stairway, as we descended the stairs he jumped and attempted to escape, I maintained my hold of him and we both ended up on the floor tumbling down eight stairs onto the lower deck .At this point Ken arrested **Suspect L**, taking him down the stairs and joining us. All three suspects were taken to Police H.Q. for questioning.

Ken Candler and I interviewed all three. The usual answers were given, denying everything and feeble excuses given as to their presence on the ship and dock estate.

When I questioned **Suspect D**, he gave false details, in fact he gave the details of another known criminal, correct name, date of birth, address and even quoted details of that persons last conviction. He was very convincing, but I knew who he was after having carried out observations on him several times and seeing his `MUG SHOT` on his Mercro file, (Merseyside criminal records office file).

I went along with his game, even filled out a charge sheet in the name given, along with a correct one. When we got to Marsh Lane Police station Bootle, our client decided he wasn't going to convince us and prior to me charging the three with, Burglary with intent to steal, he gave his correct identity to the Bridewell Sergeant. All three were bailed to appear at court on a later date BUT as we had come to expect, no further action could be taken as the ship and witnesses had sailed. This incident was later included amongst the draft charges prepared by the D.P.P.s office.

On 25th March 1981, British Transport Police, Humber Ports Division, hosted an Operation Cabinet Conference at the BTP Police Club in Hull. Not only could we discuss matters, but we could quench our thirst afterwards.

This was well attended, with representatives from over seventeen forces, including intelligence officers in particular. Details of all known suspects, their current vehicles and known associates were furnished to those in attendance, and ways of how to combat this team were discussed at length.

One interesting point here was that the Dutch officer attending revealed that they had the power to arrest suspects and detain them in custody without charge for a period of 102 days. Everyone commented how useful that would be in the UK.

Throughout that spring and summer, despite more observations and the exchange of intelligence, the problem worsened.

On 25th February 1981 we had learned that two of our suspects had been arrested in the Port of Yokohama, Japan. They were released without charge on 5th March.

On 5th April 1981, a white Rover saloon car was stop-checked by the police in Humberside. The occupants were three of our targets, who were obviously either on their way to hit a ship in the Humber Ports or had failed in their quest and were on their return journey home. The info was sketchy. What we did learn was that when the police checked the registration number on the PNC (Police National Computer) it came back still registered to Lancashire Constabulary. Subsequent follow-up enquiries revealed the car was an ex-traffic car and had been sold at auction a week or so before. Now, either that was purely coincidence or inside knowledge. I don't believe in coincidence much!

ROTTERDAM INCIDENT

On Friday 12th June 1981, the Greek vessel M.V. Alkmini was berthed in the Waalhaven in Rotterdam. The Captain left the ship with another officer to see an official. He gave his spare key of his cabin to the Superintendent, who had some work to carry out in the captain's cabin. At about 1pm that day the superintendent left the captain's cabin, closing and locking the door as he did so. Fifteen minutes later the captain returned, both going directly to the captain's cabin. The cabin door was locked, and the captain unlocked it. Whilst doing so he saw the door handle was moving. When he opened the door, he saw two men inside the cabin, he knew neither of them and asked who they were but received no answer. The men tried to push past him and leave. The captain stopped **Suspect P** but the other **Suspect Q**, ran away. He turned in the corridor and seeing his mate had been detained, ran back and kicked the captain. In consequence of this action the captain lost his hold of **Suspect P** both men then ran to the deck chased by the captain.

In the meantime, the Third officer warned the crew members that two men were attempting to escape. **Suspect P** was stopped at the gangway. **Suspect Q** jumped over the gangway onto the quayside to make good his escape and sprinted towards the direction of the dock gate. However, the ships Boatswain who was on the quayside, grabbed him and detained him. **Suspect P** who had managed to escape by now was arrested a short while later in the vicinity of the Waalhaven just outside the docks. A search of the area turned up a hire car which was parked nearby, it belonged to a car hire company in The Hague. The vehicle was unlocked, and the keys were found hidden under a mat inside. The vehicle had been hired under a false name, by someone staying in a hotel in The Hague. When **Suspect Q** was questioned, he gave false details of a person living in Liverpool. He produced a British Visitors Passport showing those details, a driving licence and medical card, all bearing the same details. **Suspect P** also furnished false details. Immediately after the arrests, the Dutch police contacted our office in Liverpool and both men were identified from tattoos etc. The hotel in The Hague was visited and the room the men had been using was searched. It was discovered a third male had been staying there but he had checked out just prior to the police arriving. The room had been booked in the third man's name. It transpired an envelope had been left at reception for the two suspects by the other man, it was found to contain a quantity of currency. There were three towels found in the room labelled "Hotel Excelsior".

When arrested **Suspect P** had a bunch of 4 keys, examination showed these were master keys made in England but for Japanese locks. The captain of the "Alkmini" confirmed they were not his. Several pathetic excuses were given by the suspects as to their presence on board. The ship was built in Japan however none of the keys found fitted the locks, the Dutch police suspected a key was thrown away by one of the suspects and not recovered.

Enquiries showed that the two suspects entered Holland on Sunday 24th May using their false passports, flying in from Manchester to Schipol airport Amsterdam. On the 25th May they hired a car in Leiden under a false name and kept the car until Friday 29th May, having travelled some 1090 Kilometres. That day, Friday 29th May, a theft was reported by a captain on board the M.V. Manthos a vessel berthed in the Waalhaven, stolen was 10.500 Dutch Florins from the captain's cabin. It appeared entry had been gained by use of a duplicate key. During this period the Belgian police, alerted the Dutch authorities that a theft of a large amount of cash had taken place during this period from a ship berthed in Antwerp harbour.

Further enquiries by the Dutch police showed that on Monday 8th June our two suspects had travelled from London Heathrow to Gothenburg in Sweden, which by the way has another large seaport. Enquiries showed they had stayed in the HOTEL EXCELSIOR, hence the towels found in their hotel room in The Hague, staying there two days. The manager of the hotel remembering they had a lot of Swedish Crowns (currency) on them. Enquiries with Interpol Stockholm showed our subjects were not known there and no thefts had been reported OR DISCOVERED, as yet. On Wednesday 10th June, the suspects flew from Sweden to Holland.

Both men were dealt with by the Dutch courts.

So, as will be noted, sometime between our suspects entering Holland on 24th May, they had returned to the UK and then flown to Sweden and then a couple of days later travelled from Sweden to Holland, arriving there on 10th June.

THE CANADIAN JOB

One lunchtime in early August 1981, I decided to go out and take a spin around some of the suspects' addresses. This time using my own car, as I did on some occasions. CID cars were easily recognisable.

It was about 12.30 p.m. I was heading along Longmoor Lane, Fazakerley, Liverpool in the direction of Kirkby, when I spotted one of our suspects standing in the doorway of a travel agent's. I continued past and parked up in a side street opposite, from where I could observe the shop doorway. After about ten minutes, he and two other known suspects left the shop and got into a car parked in the side street adjacent to the shop. I noted the car registration number as it drove off, gave it about twenty minutes just in case they returned having forgotten something, and then went into the travel agents.

Having established that the three had booked a flight to Seattle in the States, I noted all the details. The manager was most helpful, and I was assured of discretion.

In those days, prior to restrictions being lifted, anyone wishing to visit the USA had to apply for a visa to the American Embassy in London first.

During the course of enquiries and conferences attended, I had built up a vast network of contacts, police officers throughout the UK and abroad, DHSS fraud benefit officers and others, one of these contacts was a guy, let's call him Fred. He was an FBI agent, stationed at the American Embassy in London. Fred was contacted and made aware what we had discovered, that these three were due to fly to Seattle on a given date, he thanked me, confirming the visas would be granted (normally they would not have been, as their police records would have been checked) and that he would arrange for an FBI surveillance team to pick them up at the airport in Seattle upon arrival.

That way, he was hoping, our targets would be arrested as they burgled ships' cabins in the port of Seattle, which is a large port system. I guessed there would have been lots of easy pickings. The visas were granted. The targets flew to Seattle and were picked up by an FBI surveillance team. They were observed leaving the airport and boarding a Greyhound bus. However, they travelled across the river to Vancouver in Canada (a bit like going from Liverpool to Birkenhead, I suppose) and booked into a hotel there. The FBI alerted the RCMP, who in turn alerted the National Harbour's Board Police.

This in theory worked to a degree, although clearly our suspects had managed to lose the police, for a while, by changing hotel without detection, giving them sufficient time to commit offences before being arrested. However, the police now knew who they were looking for and that they would be using a hire car.

During the period our suspects were in Vancouver (21st to 27th August 1981) several offences of Burglary of ships cabins were reported.

For instance:

The M.V. Golden Miranda a Monrovian registered vessel berthed at Vancouver Wharves was attacked. On 22nd August, Captain Gunner Hansen discovered from the safe in his cabin, 840 U.S. Dollars,380 Canadian Dollars a quantity of German Marks, Belgian Francs, and Norwegian Kroner was missing, together with personal papers. Also, monies and documents belonging to a stewardess were missing. The safe had been entered, however the master key, which was hidden in the Captain's cabin, appeared not to have been disturbed.

On 23rd August Captain Lancaster the master of the Golden Miranda reported the Burglary of his cabin. He had confronted one of our suspects on board at around lunch time, the male stated he was looking for work, when questioned as to his presence on board. The Captain saw this person from the ship after explaining there were no vacancies on board. It was only later when he and his wife were about to go ashore, did they discover the theft of approx. 6.000 U.S. Dollars. The cash had been stolen from the safe situated within his cabin. Further amounts of various currencies amounting to approx. £400 was also missing from his wallet and his wife's purse, which had been left in the cabin.

Observations and searches were strengthened and following the report on 26th August of a man acting suspiciously on board the M.V. Southland Star, our three suspects were arrested in the vicinity of that ship. They were in possession of a hire car. All were arrested on suspicion of committing thefts and detained. At around 1.30pm that same day Captain Kuwada of a Japanese vessel the M.V. Matsukaze reported the theft of 82.000 Japanese Yen together with 1.530 U.S. Dollars from the ships safe in his cabin.

The subjects were searched but no monies were found in their possession, however when the police made a search of their hotel rooms a large amount of U.S. Dollar notes were found hidden wrapped within a sweater belonging to one of our suspects. No other currency was ever recovered.

It can only be presumed that our suspects had either visited a bank and the missing currency had been deposited and transferred to a bank within the UK, or monies were posted to the UK, however enquiries along these lines drew a blank.

One suspect eventually entered a guilty plea to the theft charges and received a sentence of 2 years 2 months, the other two were deported. Great work, if I say it myself. Funnily enough, the officer who dealt with them in Vancouver was a Corporal John Boulton, who was a Scouse lad (Liverpudlian) born and bred. We built up a good rapport, and when he visited relatives in Liverpool a couple of years later, he looked me up.

I recall at the time we had a CID aide in the office, Mike Trewhella, ex-MOD police, who had followed Mike Hughes and Ron Peace to us. He was a keen lad, we got on together and he didn't live far from me, so we sometimes shared car journeys. Mike was an amateur musician, played the guitar and sang a little. He was good, but he certainly chose the best career to follow. He wrote a song entitled "The Ballad of … … …," which he put to music and entertained us in the office one afternoon when "the starlings landed".

On 20th October that year, another Cabinet conference was held at Middlesbrough, this time hosted by Tees and Hartlepool Port Police. Representatives from the following attended:

River Tees Police	Sergeant Bosomworth
Port of Bristol Police	D.S. Wilson
Manchester Docks Police	Insp. Hannon and D.C. Dawes
Amsterdam River Police	D.C.I. Fred Bakker
BTP Humber Ports	D.I. Hardcastle and P.C. Beilby
Kent Constabulary Cross-Channel Liaison	D.S. Humerstone
Interpol, London	D.C. Booker
Cleveland Constabulary	D.I.s West, Stonehouse, Dobson and D.S. Wilson
Merseyside Police	D.S. McFarlane and Coffey
Cheshire Constabulary	D.S. Jack and D.S. Eyre's
No. 2 Regional Crime Squad	D.I. Riley
Port of Liverpool Police	D.I. Ralphson, D.S. Wrench and myself

For my sins I was asked to Chair the conference.

We discussed recent activities, circulation of regular bulletins and the exchange of information between forces. In order to bring new delegates up to scratch, I spoke of the modus operandi used in detail and circulated a more up-to-date set of photographs of the suspects.

Cliff Hardcastle spoke about the method the team were possibly using to dispose of the proceeds of the thefts. The matter was also discussed in detail.

It was at this point that J.R. first made mention of recent circulations in the Police Gazette and Scottish Police Gazette, seeking details of sightings of suspects and incidents of thefts, as we knew they were travelling far and wide.

It was also pointed out that prior to the enactment of the Criminal Attempts Act 1981, which became effective on 27th August 1981, we as subscribers to Operation Cabinet had to be content with dealing with suspects under certain sections of the Vagrancy Act 1824, which had recently been repealed, unless of course a substantive charge could be brought under the Theft Act.

THE HOLYHEAD INCIDENT

On 26th October 1981, a Greek vessel berthed at the port of Holyhead, North Wales, was attacked one lunchtime and over £6,000 in sterling together with a quantity of US dollars was stolen from the safe in the Captain's cabin. The Captain had closed his safe door but had failed to lock it when he left his cabin. The theft was discovered around 1 p.m. that day.

Enquiries on the dockside were made, and it was discovered a dockside employee had seen a dark-coloured Rover car near the ship. British Transport Police were alerted, who in turn informed North Wales Police. As a result, at around 3 p.m. that afternoon a police motorcyclist keeping a watch out near Hawarden, on the main A road leading to Liverpool, spotted a vehicle fitting the description with three males onboard. The vehicle was stopped, and two males were arrested, but one made good his escape, running off into a nearby housing estate. No monies were recovered, but two of our main suspects were in custody. A search of the vehicle proved negative except for a journal of commerce newspaper, which listed the daily shipping movements for UK ports.

The vital piece of evidence here was Forensic, the suspect's clothing had been taken from them and sent to the Home Office Forensic Science laboratory at Chorley Lancashire for analysis. Traces of Alumina were found in significant quantities on that clothing, furthermore it was found to be entirely consistent as a match, to the Alumina being discharged from the ship, proving both suspects had been at the scene of the Burglary in Holyhead.

The suspects were charged and eventually received custodial sentences. The third man was never identified, nor was any money recovered.

In November that year, three of our suspects were arrested in Le Havre, France, on suspicion of committing thefts from ships cabins. They were held in custody for several weeks but later released without charge.

THE DECISION THAT SET THE WHEELS IN MOTION.

In early 1982, I showed the files that I had compiled on each suspect for the past three years to J.R., suggesting we now consider bringing charges of conspiracy to burgle ships' cabins, throughout the UK and elsewhere, against the main players.

He agreed, that there now appeared to be sufficient evidence to warrant a full-blown operation and took the files to Jim Irvine, the Detective Chief Supt., for consideration.

Jim agreed with J.R. and in turn took the idea to the then Chief Constable Bill Donaldson a fellow Scotsman (Edwin Post having retired). Donaldson was an ex West Midlands Police A.C.C. The Chief gave the go-ahead and instructed us to prepare a report for submission to the DPP (Director of Public Prosecutions) in London.

A small office was set aside opposite the Chief Constable's office on the top floor at Police HQ, Gladstone Dock. We had by this time moved buildings, and I was put on the operation full time.

There was Ken Candler, J.R. and me. Ken and I began listing incidents and creating incident files.

My initial job was to create a "legend" as Jim called it. For those of you who have not got a clue what this is, let me explain, as best I can.

(Don't forget there were no computer programs or software in those days. Everything was done manually with pen and paper.)

I would take a lined piece of A4 paper and make the lines stand out more by going over with a Black pen. Then I drew lines coming down, so they formed more or less squares. Along the top or header there were columns, one for an incident number and one for a date, the date being directly under the incident number and one for the type of incident, abbreviated as, PS (for positive sighting) T (for theft) S.O. (suspicious occurrence) V.A. (vehicle acquisition) etc. At the side of the paper, the main seven suspects' names were listed going down, one above the other, so when an incident occurred, a number was given to it (entered at the top), and the date of the incident was entered below that number. You then ran your finger down below, and looking at the suspects' names on the left (say there were two involved) you put an symbol in the square(s) which appertained to the suspect concerned (see Figure 3)

There was also a separate Legend, which helped identify subjects' vehicles and link them to particular incidents.

That then allowed easy reference as to date, location, car registration number and suspects involved. Then if you went to the filing cabinet and took out the relevant file identified by the incident number, all the information and statements were there to refer to.

We had acquired two large filing cabinets and started creating files which corresponded to the Legend or graph, call it what you will. In each file would be the intelligence for that incident together with any statements taken at the time or in relation to that occurrence, which could be used in evidence.

Each page of the Legend was pinned onto the office wall. It was not long before the paper stretched right around the small office.

It was obvious that we were soon going to outgrow that small office.

Figure 3.

OPERATION 'CABINET'

Key

T.	....	Theft
S.O.	....	Suspicious Occurrence
P.S.	....	Positive Sighting
V.A.	....	Vehicle Acquisition
V.S.	....	Vehicle Sale
V.H.	....	Vehicle Hire
P.A.	....	Passport Application
H.P.	....	House Purchase
	....	Suspect Involved
A.	....	Arrest
A.C.	....	Arrest and Charged
W.	....	Warned
CON.	....	Conviction
DIS.	....	Discharged at Court
DEP.	....	Deported

Figure 3. cont-d

INCIDENT	721	722	723	724	725	726	727	728	729	730	731	732	733	734	735	736	737	738
TYPE.	T	P.S.	P.A.	T	P.S.	T	P.S.	V.A.	T	T	P.S.	T	T	T	S.O.	V.S.	V.A.	P.S.
DATE.	20 5 81	20 5 81	22 5 81	23 5 81	23 5 81	29 5 81	30 5 81	1 6 81	1 6 81	1 6 81	8 6 81	9 6 81	11 6 81	11 6 81	12 6 81	18 6 81	20 6 81	22 6 81
VENUE.	ROTHERHAM	LIVERPOOL	LIVERPOOL	JARROW	LIVERPOOL	ROTHERHAM	BOOTLE	BOOTLE	SCUNTHORPE	BLYTHE	BOOTLE	LIVERPOOL	LIVERPOOL	ROTHERHAM	ROTHERHAM	BOOTLE	LIVERPOOL	LIVERPOOL
VEHICLE.		45			46		29	47			29					41	49	44
															A.C. / CON			
															A.C. / CON			

THE BERMUDA BLAB

Whilst we were still occupying the small office, Bill Donaldson, our Chief Constable (who had been nicknamed Big Daddy due to his physique; he looked very much like Big Daddy the wrestler and must have weighed about 22 stone), attended a conference of the International Seaports and Airports Police in Bermuda in April that year (1982).

It came to our notice that the *Daily Mail* newspaper carried a short story covering this, referring to him informing the conference that his force (us, the Port of Liverpool Police) was carrying out an investigation into an international gang of Liverpool based burglars and had been working on it for four years. Furthermore, a list of names was being passed to Interpol. He also stated that the suspects were known to have been active in America, Canada, Japan and Europe. (See Figure. 4)

Thank God he did not divulge any more or that a file was being prepared for submission to the DPP.

JR was not best pleased, and it was either he or Tony Wrench who called it "The Bermuda Blab".

One Monday morning, just after the Chief returned from his jollies in Bermuda, I opened up the office, propping the door open. With it being a small room, it got quite warm. I started work, and just then J.R. came in, fag in mouth, holding a brew. He shut the door, lent over the desk, and in a low voice whilst pointing towards the Chief's office said, "He's going to shout for his driver soon (who was called Bill and worked in a nearby office) to bring his car to the front of the building."

J.R. then proceeded to explain that he had caused three handwritten letters to be sent to the Chairman of the Police Authority, the Chairman of the Mersey Dock and Harbour Company, and the Chief Constable of Merseyside Police, each identical letter being anonymous and handwritten, purporting to be from the elderly widow of a senior detective from Merseyside Police expressing her disbelief that the Chief had made public the facts about our investigation, thus tipping the villains off, as it were.

The door was then propped back open and, sure enough, after about half an hour the cry could be heard, "Bill get the car, were going out." We smiled, J.R. winked, and we carried on with the paperwork.

Nothing more was said and we, of course did not hear any more about the matter.

The Chief wasn't that bad, at least when he joined us at `Starling Time, ` as he did some afternoons, he would contribute by bringing a part bottle of Scotch, mind you there was never more than half a dozen, wee drams in it.

Throughout the year offences were still being committed both in the UK and abroad. There are obviously too many, to list here. However, as you read on, I will list a few in chronological order to give you an insight into what was taking place.

There were details of sightings and arrests coming in from Belgium via Cliff Hardcastle's office (BTP) Humber Ports. They had a reasonable line of liaison with the police in Antwerp.

We did over the years attempt to cement a better relationship with the Belgium Police, but they failed to respond accordingly. This was somewhat frustrating, to say the least. For example, we eventually learned two of our team had been arrested in Antwerp. They were found to be in possession of ships' cabin door keys. The Belgians eventually released them without charge. If we have been contacted we could have identified those keys from a burglary some months earlier.

Figure 4

Search for a gang of pirates on the dole

From PETER BURDEN in Bermuda

A GANG of British seamen are being hunted for ship robberies all over the world.

The pirates are mainly unemployed seamen from the Merseyside area who have netted so much from robbing cabins they are known to fly out to major ports for fresh raids.

They operate in threes and one team is thought to be involved in the murder of a ship's captain in Houston, Texas, the Chief Constable of the Port of Liverpool, Mr William Donaldson said yesterday.

Mr Donaldson told the annual conference of the International Association of Airports and Seaports in Bermuda that the thieves were active in America, Canada, Japan and the Philippines as well as Europe.

With many crew members paid in cash, ships were virtually floating banks but had very lax security, said Mr Donaldson.

The thefts had involved up to £500,000 a time but the total amount was not disclosed.

Mr Donaldson said that after a four-year investigation a list of 25 names had been drawn up and were to be given to Interpol. But some arrests had already been made.

Excerpt from Daily Mail, referred to as 'The Bermuda Blab'

Four

ENQUIRIES IN HOLLAND

Enquiries in Holland

We beavered away, me creating more paperwork and sticking the decoration around the office wall in our now larger office that we had been allocated further down the corridor. At least the location was good, away from Donaldson's prying eyes and right next to the toilet, so life was easier when our back teeth began to float after copious brews. We did go through quite a few cups of tea.

By this time Ken Candler had left the force and had taken up a position with the I.C.A.C. in Hong Kong (the Independent Commission Against Corruption). Ken wrote to me several times asking how things were proceeding and updating us on his life in Hong Kong. I did miss Ken.

Before he left for Hong Kong, we had really started to decorate the Cabinet Office. J.R. Ken and myself discussed the idea of obtaining evidence from the Dutch Police, regarding, Thefts in Amsterdam and Rotterdam, also the possibility of visiting Holland to obtain this, together with witness statements from Dutch officers regarding the arrests of our suspects there. This idea was put to the Chief, he agreed to allow us to travel to Holland and pursue enquiries there. Arrangements were made and Ken and I travelled to Holland by North Sea Ferries from Hull. D.I. Cliff Hardcastle, British Transport Police at Hull, had arranged the passage for us, and our contact Fred Bakker,

Commandant of the Recherchegroep, Rijkspolitie (C.I.D. Dutch National Police), had arranged accommodation at a lovely little hotel called the Oswelski near to Amsterdam centre, the husband of the lady that ran it was a retired officer and it was an I.P.A. member hotel.(International Police Association).

Ken and I drove over to Hull one afternoon, we met Cliff Hardcastle and some lads from his office prior to boarding the ferry for the overnight crossing to Rotterdam. Once on board we located our cabin, had a few drinks, and then enjoyed a meal before retiring for the night.

Upon arrival in Rotterdam the following morning, at around 7 a.m. local time, we were met by a Dutch Detective, Eef Krabbendam, with whom I struck up an immediate rapport. Eef was very friendly type and drove us to Amsterdam to meet Fred Bakker. All I can say is we got there in one piece. I wasn't used to that type of skilful fast driving, certainly not in Liverpool and furthermore we were driving on the wrong side of the road! On arrival in Amsterdam, we were taken to the H.Q. building of the Rijkspolitie te water, an old Victorian stone type building situated on the harbour front. We ascended a staircase, which led to the floor where Fred's office was situated. Eef left us in the hands of Fred Bakker, the Commandant of the Criminal Investigation Branch. I can picture it now Fred was sat behind a large desk, he was a short guy really, fair haired, thinning a little, gold rimmed spectacles, wearing a light-coloured suit. and you certainly would not have guessed he was a copper. He rose from his seat and greeted us, arranging for some coffee to be brought in and then we had a long chat about the operation and our thoughts and plans, then it was lunch in the police canteen, meatballs with gravy, a bit different from fish and chips or the stodge served up at Marsh Lane Police Canteen, Bootle, but boy was it tasty.

In the afternoon Fred gave Ken and me a guided tour of Amsterdam docks and showed us some sights. That evening we were entertained to a Chinese banquet, the like of which I shall never experience again. The restaurant had set out a long table in a private room upstairs. There was Fred, Ken, me and another Dutch detective, Theo, Fred's driver.

We were all well-spaced out (just like the social distancing we are experiencing now; I am writing this during the coronavirus outbreak of April 2020). Well, we had to be, the table was that long, and no exaggeration here, there must have been over twenty different dishes laid out with large bowls of rice. It truly was a banquet fit for a king, and how Fred arranged it (cost-wise) I don't know, but I have my suspicions this was done as a favour to him by the owner, as no money was seen to exchange hands. Mind, by the end of the evening we were all a little worse for wear.

The next morning after breakfast (still can't get used to boiled ham and cheese for breakfast), Theo, Fred's driver, collected us from the hotel, and we drove to Police HQ.

There we began work sifting through files of evidence, deciding what evidence we were shown that we could include in our operation. We needed to show and prove the activities of the team in Holland. We amassed quite a lot of paperwork, statements and files of evidence showing when some of our suspects had actually been arrested and dealt with by the Dutch. This was great evidence it showed the extent of thefts that had taken place in Holland, some of which we could include in our conspiracy file against the "Magnificent Seven" as they later became known.

That evening, we were taken to a distillery, basically a small bar in the centre of Amsterdam, situated on a Canal Street, overlooking the water, where they sold the Dutch version of gin, called jenever. The distillery was situated behind it. The drink was a little fiery for my palate. Anyway, after a couple, followed by several glasses of Oranjeboom lager chasers, we went for a meal at a traditional Dutch restaurant just off Dam Square, if I remember correctly!

I ordered what was on the menu as (if my spelling is correct) "roast beuf". It was thinly sliced and came with a selection of veg. It tasted good and I quaffed some red wine to wash it down.

It was only afterwards that Fred, without expression, asked how I had enjoyed the horse meat. I replied, "It was very tasty." To this day I have no idea if he was joking or not, and I didn't show any problems with it, thinking to myself, well that was a first.

The following morning Theo collected us from our hotel. We met up with Fred and collected the paperwork, we needed to take back with us. Included in this was a large book comprising of over 250 pages of intelligence he had made up for us detailing every incident thought to relate to our suspects.

The only problem it was in Dutch. I could make out some of the content but most of it really was "double Dutch". Then Fred decided he was going to treat us to lunch before we left.

As he drove us towards Volendam an old picturesque fishing village, we passed through the Dutch countryside, you couldn't help but notice how flat the land was, the view across the many farmers fields into the distance, was amazing, crop after crop could be seen, with the odd line of trees as boundary markers.

Lunch was on the seafront at a lovely little restaurant, on the banks of the Zuiderzee, a very large inland body of water. The area really is beautiful, little brightly coloured fisherman houses that have been well preserved. (Since that initial visit I have returned several times on holiday, taking a ferry across from Volendam to Marken, another well-preserved little Dutch fishing village.) Following lunch, we made our way back to Amsterdam.

Later that day Ken and I returned to the Port of Rotterdam for our return journey to the UK, but not before Eef Krabbendam kindly took us to see some windmills.

BACK IN LIVERPOOL

Once I had been able to digest the intelligence book that Fred Bakker had handed to me in Amsterdam, with assistance from a lovely guy, Charlie Vink, a dutchman and retired businessman, living in Liverpool, who translated it. I was able to grasp that vast amounts of currency had been stolen from ships cabins between 1976 and 1981 in both Rotterdam and Amsterdam. A lot being from safes, situated in the Captains cabins.

For instance.

U.S. Dollars	213.452
Dutch Guilders	241.516

Plus, varying other amounts in 42 different currencies.

This amount, which was recorded between those years as above, together with the other thefts that occurred later was a vast amount of cash, especially when by the end of the operation in 1984 we had also added the total of UK known thefts and thefts from France, Germany, Sweden, Canada and elsewhere.

When I looked at a period in the Dutch book, between May 1977 and September 1981 I could see there were numerous thefts that had occurred from not only Captains cabins but also from other officers' cabins, large amounts of currency had been left in desk drawers etc.

Here is a list of thefts from Captains safes alone, recorded in Holland, in that period.

9.6.80	6.500 US Dollars, 6500 French Francs, 3282 Belgium Francs and other mixed currency.
3.10.80	5996 US Dollars, 6800 French Francs, 70,000 Japanese Yen, £45, 240 D. Marks.

4.10.80	2190 US Dollars, 2152 French Francs.
24.10.80	4483 US Dollars, 10.175 French Francs.
26.10.80	4700 US Dollars
28.1.81	3300 US Dollars, 45 Canadian Dollars, 6500 Greek Drachma and other amounts of currency
31.1.81	18.891 US Dollars, 280.000 Japanese Yen.
2.2.81	13.000 US Dollars
5.2.81	4580 French Francs
17.2.81	8500 US Dollars
17.8.81	24.540 US Dollars, 117.000 Japanese Yen and other small amounts of currency.
30.9.81	2670 US Dollars.

All the above thefts were from safes, housed within the Captains cabins, either the safe key had been left in a drawer etc. within the cabin or in some instances a master key had been used.

In between the above listed offences occurring, a further 65 thefts from Captains and officers' cabins had been reported, where money had been taken from desk drawers etc.

This appears to be the period when the perpetrators had begun to specialise in gaining access to safes.

Prior to this period and from 1976, there had been over 150 reported thefts of currency from Captains and officers' cabins, in various Dutch ports and it was known that some of our suspects had been in Holland on several occasions during this period.

Following liaison with ourselves in Liverpool, our colleagues in Holland began to realise they were being visited quite frequently by what had become a team of Liverpudlian specialist International Burglars.

From the many reported thefts that had occurred in Holland, which were contained in the book that Fred had given me, I have added the following incident, to give you some idea of what was occurring there.

A Panamanian vessel, the Silver Star, was berthed at "Wilhelminakade Quay", Amsterdam.

At 17.30 hrs on 17th August 1981 the Captain locked his cabin door and went ashore. He returned in the early hours of the morning of the next day. He found his cabin door unlocked, being obviously a little drunk he went to sleep. At 08.00 hrs he went to pay his crew wages but found the safe, which was a large type money box, described as 37.6 cm x 35.0 cm x 40 cm with a key and combination system was missing from his cabin. The safe had not been secured in place.

The key was in his possession and the spare key with the Chief Engineer.

Enquiries were made on board and the Rijkspolitie attended. Enquiries showed that the previous evening two white males who spoke English came on board allegedly trying to sell watches.

Further enquiries were made, and suspects photographs shown to the crew without good result.

The safe contained 24.540 US Dollars, 117.000 Japanese Yen and an unknown amount of Ghanese currency.

The culprits obviously had a master key to gain access to the cabin but upon being unable to locate any safe key in the cabin, decided to take the safe. We had been made aware that our team of suspects had associates, who were living in Holland, one can only presume that with some outside assistance entry was gained to the safe, after all, they couldn't really take the safe back to the hotel room to force it open.

As files were created, J.R. would in chronological order, add paragraphs to his draft DPP report, showing extracts of evidence and circumstances.

We would then double-check to ensure we had the statements to back up the evidence for each file.

I can picture him now, suit jacket on, he very rarely took it off, black biro in hand, cup of tea at his side and a fag either in his other hand or smouldering away in the ash tray on his desk. I smoked a pipe in those days, so I'm afraid the office by mid-morning became rather hazy, to say the least.

By now, the time had come to further more liaison with other forces, making visits, taking or obtaining witness statements, not only from police personnel but from other witnesses, such as car salesmen who had sold cars to the suspects, ships' agents etc.

Since the outset of taking an interest in the team, I had always driven around the suspects' home addresses (as previously mentioned), collating registration numbers of any cars parked outside or nearby.

This exercise was usually carried out on my way into work of a morning, around 7.15 a.m. to 7.45 a.m. I would give Tony Wrench the details, and he would carry out a PNC (police national computer) check on them. This might show the last owner having notified the DVLA that the vehicle had been sold. If this was the case it usually meant the car had recently been purchased by our suspects, and I would then make the necessary enquiries obtaining the ownership trail (via the DVLA) and obtaining a statement from what usually turned out to be an auction house or car dealer from where the car had been purchased. This helped to show cash purchases and expenditure etc. That statement then went into the incident file in our office. As you can imagine, the suspects didn't keep a car for long (for obvious reasons), so there were quite a few statements that had to be obtained.

I had a great contact in Merseyside Police OSD (operational support division), which was a team of Bobbies based at St Anne's Street Police Station in the city, who helped. I kept my contact fully briefed of any suspect car details. He would put a marker on the PNC, so if one of these vehicles was stopped and checked anywhere in the UK by the police, it would read words to this effect: "Suspect cabin thieves blah blah, please obtain details of occupants and inform …, my contact …," who in turn fed the information though to our office, Tony entering it into his system first, then passing it to me.

Tony would also have markers put on PNC via Merseyside Police C.I.S.

This meant we were able to monitor their movements to a degree, if the vehicle was stopped, the officer would note the details of the driver and any passengers. This was most important of all, it helped prove association between the suspects, who was with who on a given date and where. All this info, together with statements, was then entered into the system back in the office and another incident file created.

L to R
Ken Candler, J.R. and the author 1982

Pictured L to R
Plain clothes section, British Transport Police 1972.
Bill Coverley, the author, Paul Freel, Terry Badger, Dog Handler Bob Farmer and Jim Harvey. Photo courtesy of Paul Freel

Pictured L to R
John Ralphson, Rod Bradley and the Author

Five

CONFERENCES AND LIAISON

Conferences and Liaison

From the start of Cabinet, we had a very close relationship with BTP Humber Ports Division. This came about as our two locations had been hit the most, and liaison between us was good, partly because Cliff, the D.I. there, liked to come over to Liverpool on a working "jolly". Of course, a few pints were quaffed down with lunch in the Merton Hotel in Bootle and partly as I was ex-BTP. I struck up a great friendship with a guy, Rod Bradley, a Detective who was stationed at Grimsby Docks, whereas Cliff was at Hull Docks, but he oversaw the four Humber Ports, Hull, Grimsby, Immingham and Goole. Rod and I are still good friends to this day. When we speak on the phone or meet up, we always seem to refer to our days working together, and Rod starts laughing and reminiscing about some of the strokes we pulled off. I bumped into a former colleague Steve McDonald a few years ago, he referred to those days in the job, as like being at "St Trinian's". I wished Rod and myself had worked together on a more permanent basis. We thought alike, and I suppose you could say we had the same police mentality. Throughout my career there were not many colleagues I would have trusted, but Rod, Ken Candler, Mick Hughes and J.R. were in the top few.

I DIGRESS AGAIN HERE

During the early part of 1982, we entertained officers from Cheshire Constabulary Criminal Intelligence Section. This was arranged via Tony Wrench, who was ex-Cheshire County before being swallowed up into Merseyside Police during the amalgamations in the 1970s.

The D.I., Gordon Hutcheson, and a couple of his colleagues came over for lunch. I arranged a visit to the Petty Officer's mess onboard a visiting submarine, *HMS Conqueror,* which was berthed in Seaforth Dock. We went onboard and as usual were very warmly received. One thing about British warships, submarines included, they carry a good stock of beer, not like our colonial cousins from across the pond. Following a few beers and sandwiches, Hutch decided he needed a pee. He asked me where the toilet was. I pointed him in the direction along the boat's main corridor but omitted to tell him toilets on any Royal Navy ship are not marked "Toilets" or "Gents". The sign above the doorway reads "Heads".

Hutch returned looking very relieved and sat down. Just then, red warning lights were flashing. There was a little confusion as some of the P.O.s went to investigate, but the problem was solved. The phantom pee'r, in his infinite wisdom, failing to locate the toilet (sorry, "heads") had opened two small aluminium doors and upon seeing a mesh tray proceeded to relieve himself into this.

Now, the only problem was he had opened the doors to a ventilation shaft that went straight down to the torpedo room, so he had christened a couple of torpedoes. The trouble was there were damp sensors stuck to the torpedoes. Bingo, the alarm went off. The lads were OK about it and laughed it off, and we continued socialising.

Now, on the morning of Monday 3rd May 1982, my phone rang in the office. The voice at the other end was Hutch, who said, "Paul, have you heard about the *Belgrano* being sunk by that submarine we were on?" (This was during the Falklands war. The *Belgrano* was an Argentine Navy light cruiser, which was near to the Falkland Islands.) I replied, "Yes." He went on to say, "Just think, I might have pissed on the torpedo that sank it." Then we both burst out laughing.

Incidents kept occurring throughout the UK and elsewhere, Holland especially.

On 4th November 1982 I attended a Criminal Intelligence Officers Conference (representing Operation Cabinet) which was held at H.M. Prison, Wakefield. There were delegates there from various Northern Police Forces. I updated them on the progress being made with the operations. Now, I recall the day before I went, the Chief, Bill Donaldson, who was OK but liked to let you know he was "the Chief", handed me the keys to a new vehicle our force was trying out. I had seen a uniform inspector using it as a supervision car. He said, here you are young man, take that tomorrow and let me know how you think it handles.

The day after the conference I took the keys back to the admin office. The Chief was in there and he asked what I thought of the car. I said, "Well it's OK, Sir, but it doesn't really hold the road at 40 mph around roundabouts." He immediately went red, but before he could explode, he realised I was smiling, so he laughed it off.

On 12th October 1982, an Introductory Report broadly outlining the problem was submitted to the Director of Public Prosecutions. This included broad extracts of evidence, which included details of over forty incidents.

There were three booklets in all, plus the report, the legend showing main suspects, the index of vehicles used by the suspects and the schedule of the associates of the suspects. We concluded, that we had details of over 750 offences being committed over the past five years, involving the theft of over £800,000 in the UK alone and over 1,000 incidents being recorded.

The Chief attached a covering letter explaining matters and stressing the fact that Interpol were wanting to issue a Green warning notice to have the suspects identified.

The DPP's office rang asking if we could visit their offices on 9th November to discuss the matter more in depth, but in the meantime, we were to submit an "extract of evidence".

This was completed and forwarded on 2nd November.

On Tuesday 9th November myself and J.R. left Lime Street Station, Liverpool on the 7 a.m. train bound for London. On arrival at London Euston Station we were met by a detective from the British Transport Police (I had arranged this through Dennis Ward, D.I., BTP HQ), who drove us to the DPP's office and back. This took the pressure off having to use the London underground, I really didn't look forward to having to use that mode of transport, everyone cramped together and looking rather poe faced and unfriendly, staring into the window opposite, no expression.

Upon arrival we were met by two gentlemen, one being the Assistant Director.

We were thanked for attending, and comment was made upon the quality of the reports submitted (that was down to J.R., there was no one better to formulate such a report), particularly stressing the format and obvious vast amount of work involved, which made their task of understanding the file much easier.

It was during these discussions that it was decided to stick to the main seven players that we had singled out, the leaders, as the Assistant Director called them. He went on to say that by achieving convictions against those and hopefully obtaining lengthy custodial sentences, this would act as a deterrent to the others.

The Assistant Director agreed to instruct Counsel to look at the matter further. At this point I jumped in with both feet and asked if we could have Brian Leveson, a young Liverpool-based barrister, to be instructed. I saw J.R. look at me. I had not mentioned this to him previously, and he had no idea who I was referring to. When we had left the DPP's offices and were on the return journey to Euston Station, he asked "Who is Leveson?" I told him that I had picked up on the name when I was working with the RCS (Regional Crime

Squad) on a job. Eddie Rimmer and John Clark couldn't speak highly enough of him. They held him in high esteem. It was mentioned he was a brilliant up-and-coming prosecution barrister. All J.R. said was, "Well, he will need to be good on this one. "Funnily enough, as things transpired Brian Leveson, prosecuted a case for us a little later that year. This was a one-off case of Burglary against a suspect, who was not in the `A` team, he had been identified on fingerprint evidence alone, having stolen a significant amount of cash from the ships safe of a Japanese vessel, the M.V. Geiko Maru, on Tuesday 8th June 1982, whilst berthed at the Tranmere Oil terminal, Birkenhead. He went onto enter a plea of not guilty, thinking we would not be able to arrange for the complainant, the Captain to return for the trial. Well guess what, he was wrong, Captain Takeda flew in from Italy, gave his evidence and we obtained a successful guilty verdict, the offender receiving a lengthy custodial sentence. This incident is later referred to in the final chapter.

I sit back now and think, we probably helped Brian Leveson on his climb up the legal ladder, to become Sir Brian Leveson, Lord Justice Leveson, gaining his Knighthood and later to chair the phone hacking enquiry.

The following day back at the office we decided to firm up the main players, double-checking the strength of incidents against them and ensuring we had all the evidence needed to back up those incidents. Anything missing would have to be chased up.

Shortly after our visit to the D.P. P's office we were asked to attend the Barristers chambers, of Brian Leveson, in Liverpool.

We there met with Mr Leveson and discussed the matter in detail, he had of course been furnished with a copy of our introductory report and had obviously digested it thoroughly.

We were instructed to proceed by gathering as much evidence as possible, I recall Mr Leveson saying, "get whatever you need".

With this in mind we spent periods of time over the next couple of weeks, on the top floor of the offices of a company which overlooked the unemployment benefits office in Park Road, Bootle, armed with a 35 mm camera and telephoto lens. The suspects were photographed as they arrived to "sign on". They would arrive sharing a car or in a taxi, the photos were to prove association, if need be.

Another conference took place at Hull on 25th November 1982, again hosted by British Transport Police. This was well attended by 58 delegates from various forces, including officers from the Dutch Police. Officers also attended from Belgium, as they had for a while been experiencing problems in Antwerp Harbour and had on occasions arrested some of our suspects. I updated the conference with the up-to-date intelligence regarding team members, and J.R. spoke about the current state of the master file of evidence that was being prepared for the DPP.

J.R. went on to explain that in most of the convictions under the Vagrancy Act (i.e., Reputed Thief Loitering or Suspected Person Loitering), the offender was given a small fine or a short sentence, which was no real deterrent.

We then spoke about bringing the case of conspiracy against the suspects and J.R. updated the conference on our visit to the D.P.P.s office. The definition of Section 5 of the Criminal Attempts Act 1981 in relation to Conspiracy was discussed in detail.

Cliff Hardcastle, the D.I. of BTP Humber Ports, spoke about what method the team were using to get the stolen currency back to Liverpool. We didn't know, if they risked driving back with it in their possession or if they posted it to a Liverpool address. Obviously, if they nicked the currency out of bank opening hours, it presented a problem for it to be paid in at a bank near the locus of the offence, say for instance in the Humberside area. So, would they risk driving back with any stolen currency in their possession?

Before the conference business closed, J.R. stood up and read the following little "Piece" he had composed:

> *"There is nothing new in our line of work – just different ways of doing it. And to illustrate how little things change, one only has to turn to the scriptures:*
>
> *I refer to the book of St Paul, Chapter 14, verse 27, which says:*
>
> *And in the beginning, there were those who sought to conspire and do evil and they went from their houses*

to many places, to many shores and unto other lands, where they gathered unto themselves those things which did not belong to them and the people were much troubled.

Then there came amongst them the disciples who called themselves the "Police" and they cried out of one accord – Be not afraid, we shall deliver you from this evil and give testament from the great temples and they who do evil shall be punished.

And the disciples went among the flocks and gathered sayings which they transcribed into writings (statements).

But there were certain scholars who mocked the disciples saying, "It will not come to pass"

But the disciples wilted not and gathered all their writings and took them to the great tabernacle, where the Lord, who was known unto them as the DPP, received them into his house, where they rested, and after they had rested, he said unto the disciples, "Lo and behold!"

I say unto you, seek those who mocked you and sayeth unto them, "Oh ye of little faith," and return to your flocks and speaketh unto them also saying that the date of judgement draws nigh and those who have committed those evil acts will be called to answer, and goodness will prevail in all our lands and you who have spread the gospel shall find great reward and there shall be rejoicing in the Good Shepherd, the Rose and Crown and Montrose.

So endeth the 4th lesson (the fourth Cabinet Conference)".

Following the conference, we set up with the post office a "mail check" on twenty-seven known addresses throughout the Merseyside area, not just the seven main players' addresses, but other known associates. This meant if a bulky envelope (possibly containing banknotes) was bound for one of the suspect's known addresses, we would be alerted early morning, meaning a search warrant could be obtained immediately and a controlled delivery set up, with us in attendance. Nothing came of that idea. However, we were informed when post from overseas was delivered, such as postcards or airmail letters, which either meant the team were writing home or another suspect was abroad. So, we knew they were in Holland, for instance, from the postage stamps or franking. That way we could tip off the Dutch police that someone appeared to be operating on their patch.

Six

J.R., A MAN'S MAN, POET AND PRANKSTER

J.R., A Man's Man, Poet and Prankster

Having now been working closely with J.R. for quite a time, I got to know him more and more as the days and weeks went by. He was a shrewd, clever old-time detective who, after being demobbed following the Second World War, had joined Liverpool City Police. Why Liverpool, when he came from East Lancashire, near Bury? Well, the love of his life, Norma, was the answer. Norma was a north-west girl and obviously wasn't for upping sticks, so Liverpool it was.

From uniform J.R. went into CID. Then in the 1960s he was a Detective Sergeant in the Liverpool City Police Commando Squad. The City of Liverpool at this time had seen a spike in crime. The then Acting Chief Constable Bert Balmer set up a squad of Detectives known as the Commando Squad. Officers were told there had to be results, criminal activities had to be supressed and villains arrested. Even in those days it became apparent that liaison between neighbouring forces was crucial. As J.R. told me, the offender may have been living in Liverpool, but even back in those days would travel into neighbouring force areas to commit crime there.

John was an absolute gentleman. I never heard him bad-mouth anyone unless they really deserved it. He was no doubt the man for the job when it came to writing reports, and that is where the tenacity for detail shone through in the DPP reports he prepared, leaving no detail out and explaining matters in simple terms that could be understood by any "degree-holding intellectual".

We often talked about police-related matters of the past, as some of you will appreciate (boring bastards, aren't we?) and of his wartime service.

I remember him telling me about being involved in a landing force in Norway during the war, his time in North Africa, and later when he was a "sniper" in Germany near the end of the war. His job, together with a spotter, was to get into a bombed-out building near the German frontline. The spotter would look for German officers, and J.R. would terminate them. The idea was to leave the German soldiers in a state of chaos.

Then he told me about the Kray brothers' incident (I suppose his claim, or one of his claims, to fame) in Liverpool.

I have read and heard various accounts on this subject, but here is what he related to me.

He had been told by a local club owner that the Krays had been in Liverpool and were looking to set up a protection racket. The club owner had been approached and was told they, the Krays, would visit again a week later for payment. J.R. was working with another Detective, Les Skinner. On the day in question, they had been overseeing a consignment of bullion onto a train at Lime Street Station. J.R. was armed with a pistol. He did not elaborate on whether Les Skinner was armed or not. I suppose he was. Anyway, later the two of them went down to the club. They sat at the bar having a drink, when in walked Reggie Kray with a minder. The club owner introduced J.R. and Skinner as detectives. It was apparently at this point that Kray said to J.R, "Me and you can do business together, gov."

After a very short time, Kray went to make a phone call from the telephone booth situated inside the club. J.R. followed, barged into the booth, drew his pistol, shoved it under Kray's chin and basically told him to fuck off out of town and don't return. The Krays left, never to return to Liverpool again. They did try it on in Manchester a short time later but more or less got the same message. As I am typing this, I am thinking that just wouldn't happen today. Imagine, the shit would hit the fan good style. There would be instant dismissals, internal enquiries and Christ knows what else. Apart from all that, there would not be anyone with the balls to just do it without seeking clearance first. I am afraid to say, no doubt, it just would not happen.

With five arrests for murder under his belt and his war time experiences, who better to sort the Krays out than him?

I asked JR what Kray's reaction was, he replied, Kray said "Your mad, and I said yes I am".

I would say John Ralphson was one of the few senior officers I ever had any respect for. To me he warranted the utmost respect above everyone else. We completely trusted each other. He would divulge matters to me that he really shouldn't have.

Not long after I had left the job, J.R. retired and invited me to his leaving do at the police club on the docks. I had arranged for Fred Bakker to fly in from Amsterdam, and I picked him up at Manchester Airport. Rod Bradley, who by then had been promoted to a uniform Sergeant at Grimsby, came over to stay with me.

We all attended his gathering one Friday afternoon. I had arranged for a kissogram to attend, so around 3 p.m. a very scantily dressed blonde female turned up. The music went on, and she sang "Happy Birthday" to him and sat on his knee for a photo to be taken (sadly, I don't have a copy).

A good time was had by all, and J.R. then descended into retirement – but not for long.

After a couple of months, he rang to inform me he was working three days a week in a Birkenhead solicitors' office, interviewing "bucks" that had been arrested and preparing a file for the defending solicitor. He explained he couldn't stand being at home full time, it was getting on his nerves.

Norma apparently held coffee mornings; some ladies came around and J.R. was asked to humour them and serve tea and biscuits etc. He said, "That was it, I thought I've got to get out of here. I can't be doing with this."

He rang me several times whilst he was working at the solicitors' office. He reckoned he had obtained more coughs from the "bucks" than any Bobby in Birkenhead, persuading the offenders to plead guilty. We laughed about that.

Some of you more experienced readers will probably understand the force on the docks was more like an old-fashioned Borough Police Force. Everyone knew everyone else and, to coin a phrase, if somebody farted you all knew. I suppose in one way that closeness helped to get things done.

J.R. would often write little pieces of poetry, which were always produced in an afternoon when "the starlings" had landed. The following are a few little snippets.

(When Jim is referred to, that's Jim Irvine. Detective Chief Supt. T.W. is Tony Weston, Harry is Harry McCauley and Tony is Tony Wrench.)

I think it was 1981 when Tom Shepherd (T.S.) the Deputy Chief Constable was made acting Chief Constable, as the then Chief Constable had retired. This left his position vacant, so Jim was made Acting Deputy Chief Constable. That in turn meant that Jim's position of Detective Chief Superintendent was vacant, so J.R. was made Acting Detective Chief Inspector. This again meant the Detective Inspector's post was vacant, so Detective Sergeant Tony Weston was made Acting Detective Inspector.

At the end of their periods of acting roles, J.R. decided it was the appropriate time to mark the occasion with a bottle. The starlings once more "landed" one Friday afternoon in the CID admin office, and of course, true to fashion, a bit of light-hearted "wit" was produced by J.R., which read as follows:

The day has come, but shed no tears,
For Jim, John and Tony
All "Acting Sirs" in higher rank, until next Monday only.
Jim took to D.C.C. like water to a duck,
Reports galore were showered on him,
But he didn't give a ….
The Admin staff, they worked so hard,
He didn't have to bawl,
His gentle Scottish burr, a goad to typist, clerk and all.
J.R., the boss, he did his whack by sitting in the chair,
The aggro came quite thick and fast,
It really wasn't fair.
But John was up to the task in hand and cared for all his men,
With velvet-covered fist he fought with T.S. now and then.
T.W. He didn't do bad,
He did his share of call outs (some say more than he ought to have).
But most of all the working men, the staff, the jacks, the cream,
They worked so well with loyalty; it all went like a dream.
So, thanking one and all we say,
Let's have a drink tonight.
Demoted we all may have been,
But we don't give a ….

TONY WRENCH'S MISDEMEANOUR

Now, Jim was a stickler for paperwork and having things done right. For example, only he or J.R. were permitted to write in the margin in the office occurrence book. Alas, Tony Wrench went and blotted his copybook. Jim did raise the subject with all. By the end of the week, the subject had eased and at Starling time on the Friday afternoon J.R. produced the following:

Not a phone was used, nor a message wrote
As the jacks hurried back melancholic. ["jacks" is an expression for detective]
Not a smile was raised, not a jest was said.
For someone was due a bollock.
No, it's not for the crime of just being late,
Nor Jack Holt's excess overtime charging.
Far worse than that, the unpardonable sin,
Tony Wrench went and wrote in the margin.
Said the boss, white and drawn, "He'll be shot come the dawn."
"This crime I can never forgive."
"Not that," cries J.R. "Not like some Russian Tsar,
To die like a dog in the morning."
"Alright then," says Jim, his face looking grim.
"He'll be let off this once with a warning,
The next offender I will never forgive,
He'll be shot without trial next morning."
The jacks looked away, there was nothing to say.
Poor Tony, with eyes full of tears,
Cried, "I don't mind the whip, the rack or thumbscrews.
But he's taken my pen for three years."

With apologies to *The Burial of Sir John Moore's after Corruna.*

Jim Irvine at the time of his retirement gave J.R. a present, and of course JR marked the occasion with a few lines of verse, read out as the "starlings landed" one afternoon.

All is revealed, read on!

AN ODE TO A MISSING BOTTLE
(Or Bovril and Ginger Don't Mix)

"There's a parcel here for us to share," said Harry with a grin,
I don't know who has sent it, but it could be from Sinn Fein.
The lads all scattered calling, "You can open it, Boss."
And if by chance it should explode there'll be no serious loss.
I examined the package carefully, but there was no ticking sound,
Then came to a conclusion, a conclusion so profound,
I called them back again, and some had gone a mile.
"You need not worry lads" I said, "I know the wrapping style.
It's from Jim, just calm your fears, there is no cause for quivers,
He's been busy with the tape again, and of course his little scissors."
As I unwrapped the parcel, they gathered around less tense.
It must be something good, they said, postage seventy pence.
[It was sixty-six pence, but that made the line too long]
Jack Holt asked, "Is that a lot?"
And Tony said, "Yes, for a Scot."
First of all, we found the car, a windmill, snow and ice,
"Our artist" (Tony) said, "It's a David Beatty painting."
And the rest of us said, "That's nice."

Then we saw the goblets box, two goblets for a toast?
"Perhaps," I said, "the champagne will come with the very next post."
But our elations were quickly changed from an anticipated thrill
When we discovered, 'neath the wrapping, a jar of Bovril.
We chorused:
Despite his seven years education here at "Merton" and at "Trinity" [reference to roads in Bootle]
And helping him till he achieved his "Docker of Divide-ity",
His further full-time studies at the Mersey Bar

He still does not know the difference between a bottle and a jar.
We will, however, persevere,
And whenever you and Pat are near
To Liverpool or in these areas,
We'd be very pleased if you'd call in to see us.
But in the we send our "Greetings"
And look forward to our future meeting.

Oh, to be in England and support an English team,
To rid oneself of Celtic, a nightmare of a dream,
Bless Merseyside supporters and their misunderstanding of the game,
But not the misbehaviours at which true Scots hang their heads in shame.
We bring the Scottish player here, well! those with some potential.
To make each of them eventually a respected football star [which rhymes with jar]
With Liverpool Football Club, to whom Europe is no bar [which also rhymes with jar].
Sportsmanship and play the game is our inherited theme,
And Liverpool will forever be THE United Kingdom team,
We applaud all sportsmen, Dalgleish, Coe and Cockle,
And it's funny how so many words rhyme with bottle.

Apart from producing little poems, I recall on one occasion, when the "starlings landed", I was presented with a mocked-up certificate in recognition of my efforts "ferreting for information" in relation to the operation.

I can honestly say that it was a privilege to have served under such a great guy. He would back his men to the hilt (not like today).

John went on to write a book entitled *Wynter*. It was about a fictional Liverpool detective, but when you read it, it's obviously based on a lot of his experiences.

We stayed friends for many years up until his death. I would visit him on the Wirral where he lived, taking him a bottle of course, and sometimes Norma would lay a snack on for my wife and me. When J.R. was admitted to hospital in around 2012, I visited him and had the shock of my life. There was this little old man lying in a hospital bed, and I must admit I did not recognise him at first. He was asleep. I sat down beside him thinking, "If he wakes up soon, fine, if not I will just leave." He woke, a smile came to his face, and he tried to adjust himself. I told him not to worry, but he insisted saying "I'll sit up for you." That remark has stuck in my mind ever since.

I didn't see J.R. after that. I did speak to him and Norma a few times on the phone, and then I tried ringing one day and the line was dead. I made enquiries and ascertained he and Norma had gone to live in Derbyshire, near his daughter. I made contact and found they were in a care home, then shortly afterwards I received a call from Lynne his daughter informing me, that he had passed away.

I made the effort and drove over to the funeral in Chesterfield. What really upset me was the fact that not one person from either Merseyside Police or the Port of Liverpool Police attended, which I thought was a total disgrace. Then I remembered an old bobby saying to me once, "Remember this lad, you are only as good as your last job." How bloody true those words were.

When his ashes were laid to rest at Little Neston church, I sadly couldn't attend but was pleased to hear that Dave Liptrot and some other retired Merseyside officers did.

By the time J.R. had retired from the Port of Liverpool Police, he had clocked up Forty years continuous service as a police officer and close to Thirty-Eight of those years as a Detective. I guess he should really be mentioned in the Guinness Book of Records.

Seven

DAILY OFFICE ROUTINE 1982 and OTHER ENQUIRIES

Daily Office Routine 1982 and Other Enquiries

I would open the office around 7.30am, first checking in the control room for any telephone or telex messages coming in from other forces, especially from the Dutch police. Should there be anything from Holland I would ring my contact Eef Krabbendam in Rotterdam. It was Eef who usually rang us, as they started their day an hour before we did. He had usually left messages for me, by the time I went into the office. If Harry Locket, who was ex Lancashire County and lived near me, was the morning uniformed Sergeant, he would always, find his way up to our office knowing I would supply him with a brew, of what my mother referred to as, `Garside's Tea`. This was a brew with a `Wee Dram in it. The term Garside's Tea, apparently came from a shop that existed in Ormskirk many, many, years ago, called Garside's, where people could obtain a brew and have a tot put in it. Harry knew I liked my morning brew this way and, in those days, most `Jacks` had a bottle in their desk drawer, purely for medicinal purposes of course!

Having dealt with any messages, I would pick up on the paperwork from where we left off the previous day. J.R. would join me, brew in hand and usually a fag in the other. If he needed bringing up to speed on overnight matters or problems we had encountered, we would discuss those. Then he would continue writing his report, me supplying the info, making sure we had cross-referenced everything correctly. By 9.30 a.m. it was bacon butty time. Either he would throw a fiver on the desk or I would pay, nipping to the canteen to acquire two rather large bacon butties (now, I know what you're thinking: cholesterol). On my way back upstairs, I would collect two brews of tea, then it was nosebag time.

Come lunchtime, which was usually taken at our local sub-office, the Merton Hotel or another local establishment that served a good pint and some grub. Sometimes we went down to the Club Ship Landfall, berthed in Bramley Moor Dock (this was a WW2 landing craft which had been converted into a floating club). I knew Brian, one of the owners, and we were made most welcome. If we had a lot to get through, it was a working lunch with a sandwich. By 1.15 p.m. we were back to the office, sooner if a quick lunch was needed. I laughed each day as his wife, Norma, thought he was on a health kick and supplied him with a lunchbox with two Ryvita biscuits, a hardboiled egg, and some ham or cheese and celery. He would open the box, take either the egg or ham, offer me the rest and then throw the remainder in the bin. He did not like to upset Norma and went along with the healthy eating idea to keep the peace. It was like when he smoked. J.R. liked nothing more than a pipe full of tobacco, but he mainly smoked fags, so Norma issued him with a cigarette holder which had some sort of filter in it. He rarely used it but kept it in his pocket. It was the Christmas CID office meal out. I think it was 1983, and we went to Thornton Hough Hotel on the Wirral. I was sat opposite J.R. and Norma. As the meal finished, I got my pipe out, and J.R. took a packet of cigarettes from his jacket pocket. He got his cigarette holder out and proceeded to load it with a fag. He saw me looking and feared I might make a comment. At that point I received a slight kick under the table followed by a shake of the head, so I commented whilst smiling and commended Norma on her actions. I could see the sigh of relief come over his face.

As previously mentioned, the suspects were using numerous different vehicles in an attempt to avoid detection and were travelling to and from the continent and further afield.

We therefore needed to prove the purchase or hire of these vehicles, the amounts paid, and any hire fees involved. In relation to air travel, the same applied: proof was needed, and statements obtained. This entailed visits to Travel agents, British Airways offices and KLM offices in Manchester.

Throughout the early part of 1982 I spent some of the time visiting auction houses, car sale rooms and car hire companies, interviewing staff and obtaining those statements and documentation.

Later that year in his Advice, Mr Leveson drew the matter of expenditure to the fore, suggesting we show, where possible, the amounts of money each suspect was spending coupled with a statement from the unemployment benefit office to show the fact that the expenditure of suspects exceeded the benefits received.

This was done and strengthened even more later, when we discovered documentation in their houses, purchase receipts, etc which went onto show the amounts of expenditure some of our suspects were incurring.

DUTCH INCIDENT, THAT NEVER OCCURRED.

One morning early in 1982 I had just signed on duty. It would have been about 8.15 a.m. when I received a telephone call from Rotterdam. It wasn't from my usual contact but another detective. He was asking for assistance and wondered if I could help. It transpired that in the early hours of that morning a flight had arrived at Schiphol Airport, Amsterdam, from the Far East. One passenger had been arrested after being found in possession of a white powder that was suspected to be heroin, concealed in a luggage case. The guy was described as white and spoke with what appeared to be an American accent. He was found to be in possession of two passports bearing his photograph and identical details. One passport was British and the other American. I was asked if I could check out the British one. I told the Dutch Officer that I would make enquiries regarding both passports, as I had a contact at the American Embassy in London.

I waited until 9am and rang my contact, the police liaison officer in the passport office in Glasgow (Glasgow was at that time the main passport office for the UK where all records were kept), and appraised him of the situation, asking if he could verify the details of the British passport. Within a very short time I received a call from him advising me that the passport details I gave him had never been issued. It was, therefore, a false passport. I then rang my FBI contact in the US Embassy, London, giving him details of the American passport.

He agreed to make enquiries and said he would ring me back. He did after about half an hour, advising me the American passport was a false one, too.

I made a brew and was just about to ring the detective in Holland, when he rang to inform me the suspect in custody had admitted – wait for it – that he was an agent working for a certain intelligence organisation, who was doing a little side-line, to supplement his income. I rang my contact straight away at the Embassy and told him what I had been told. His reply was, "Shit, this conversation never took place." I advised my contact at the passport office in Glasgow accordingly. Nothing more was heard, matter closed.

MURDER OF A SHIPS CAPTAIN AT MORGAN POINT, TEXAS, USA

During April of that year, we received an enquiry from the Sheriff's office Harris County, USA. I remember Ken Candler coming along the corridor from the Chiefs office, he had an American Police, wated poster, in his hand. It transpired that a ship's Captain had been shot dead, when he disturbed a Burglar in his cabin, on board the S.S. Tampa berthed at Barbours Cut, Morgan Point, Texas on the 19th February 1982. The poster gave full details of the crime and a photo sketch of the alleged offender.

They contacted us, as they had been made aware our operation and that our suspects were known by the National Harbours Board Police to operate in various parts of Canada, it was also suspected maybe the U.S.A. It was therefore felt feasible, that the offender in this case could be one of our team. Enquiries were made but there was nothing to link any of our suspects with this murder. The photo fit, didn't really resemble any of our team and we had no intelligence that suggested any of them were in Canada or the U.S.A. at that time, furthermore, to be honest about this, I know our team were Burglars and Thieves but I couldn't really see one of them being callous enough to commit a murder.

Eight

THE NET CLOSES IN

The Net Closes In

Throughout early 1983 we continued to create incident files and realised the time had come to concentrate on bank enquiries. Obviously, the suspects were coming into possession of numerous different currencies, so how were they disposing of it? The answer obviously lay with banks.

We created a full list of all the banks in the Merseyside area, including building societies.

In March I took out a Bankers Evidence Act Order for a branch of the Midland Bank in Liverpool. We had gleaned some intelligence that one of the suspects was known to use that bank on occasions. So, after visiting the bank and going through records of foreign currency transaction slips, I came away with several slips which had been completed bearing this suspects details, showing that an exchange of foreign currency had taken place. Each slip not only listed in detail the currency involved, date of transaction but also showed the suspect's details and bore a signature. It was obvious then that this was going to be an avenue worth pursuing in relation to all our targets. In fact, on this one occasion, the amount and type of currency exchanged matched that of some currency from a burglary of a ship's cabin a few days earlier.

That month (March) I received a letter from Ken Candler in Hong Kong, Ken had by this time settled into his post with the I.C.A.C in Hong Kong (The Independent Commission against Corruption). I will now include extracts from his letter.

Dear Paul and Family,

First of all, excuse the typewriter but I`m at work and it's much easier to get through a letter quickly rather than write it. The sea is immediately below our apartment, in fact I could dive into the sea from our balcony, the view is tremendous – across to several small islands with ships of all kinds passing below.

Thanks for your letters and photos. I`ll bet (here he names a suspect) was pleased when he got his sentence. Your name would be passed around The, ... Public House in Bootle, with some pleasing remarks!!! From what you say it just shows that with some persistence, what can be achieved. (Ken was referring to the successful prosecution of a suspect for the Burglary of a Captain's cabin, this incident is referred to in chapter 5 re the M.V. `GEIKO MARU.`

It's a bit disappointing having to prove the thefts though. However, I would think that you will come up with enough English names to prove a system over the years. (By this he meant showing a pattern used by the offenders). I remember that we had several statements from a various officer already. Does the thinking also apply to thefts in Amsterdam and Rotterdam etc?? Whatever, you do -DO NOT GIVE UP THE FIGHT- we put in far too much effort or at least you did to let it slide now. Just think what our prime suspect and the others would be like if nothing further happened. In any case I once promised him that I would knock on his door early one morning and he would know then that his time had come. Maybe now it won't be me but now it must be you.

I miss the place a little. We deal with Hong Kong Police corruption only in our section. We also have several Chinese lads on our section, I get on fine with them. They call me KEN JAI, meaning young Ken. I like nothing better than to get out early in a morning, into the New Territories and lock up an offender.

Ken then closed his letter asking to be remembered to JR and the others.

Ken was right, I had no intention of giving up and knew that if he had still been with us and not in Hong Kong, he would be leading from the front.

In April that year, myself and J.R. visited British Transport Police HQ, London, where the D.I. in the Criminal Intelligence Section entertained us, and we were able to discuss the complexity of this case.

Tony Wrench, J.R. and I visited the RCIO (Regional Criminal Intelligence Office) at Greater Manchester Policy HQ, where we discussed matters with John Robbins, the boss there updating him on our operation. John Robbins was a very obliging guy, a good friend of Tony Wrench and tried to assist as much as possible, gathering intelligence for us.

A further meeting with the DPP was held on Wednesday 4th May 1983, when we were introduced to Miss Eleanor

Phillips of that office, who had been appointed our case manager. We brought Miss Phillips up to date as to how the file was being prepared and the further enquiries we needed to carry out, together with details of additional statements required. Soon afterwards we furnished Brian Leveson with a draft file of evidence and covering report, which JR had composed.

At this stage J.R. had made provisional plans to carry out the raids on the seven suspects' home addresses in early June, and we decided D-Day would provisionally be Wednesday 8th June.

Not long after this we had supplied Mr Leveson with a draft of evidence, and on 31st May he in return furnished us with a large written Advice, consisting of several pages, in relation to the compilation of a file of evidence, detailing how the file should be edited and presented prior to the committal stage.

In mid-May we had discussions with Assistant Chief Constable McGregor of British Transport Police. Sometimes I felt we were like jugglers trying to keep all the balls up in the air at once, keeping everyone involved up to speed.

It became obvious by this time that we needed to strengthen the team in the office. J.R. asked Les Evans, a retired Merseyside Detective who had joined our force some years earlier, to come onboard as the Exhibits Officer. Les was a truly cracking guy and was good with paperwork, and that was what was required: someone who had the patience and could systematically put a file of exhibits together in an order that could be followed. He was a tall guy, average build, sharp featured and always wore a suit, with his tie held in place with a tie pin or it was tucked into his trouser front, Les always looked smart, he smoked like a chimney though, so with him in our office, today's standards of health and safety went out the window. Les would sit at his desk writing away, I can picture him now and the thing I found amusing was, when he was really concentrating whilst scribing away, he would hold his tongue out of the corner of his mouth and somehow rotate it. I don't think he really knew he was doing this; it did make me smile.

One Friday lunch time around 11.45 a.m. in mid-May, J.R., who had been bursting into realms of `Enid Blyton`, all morning, announced he was going for a swim with Tony Wrench to Oriel Road baths in Bootle (this was a twice-weekly ritual, they liked to keep fit). So off they went. I thought, right I know what I need to do. We still needed another person to work closely with me on these enquiries (someone I knew I could trust and rely on). I rang Dennis Ward, the D.C.I. at BTP HQ, London and enquired what the possibility was of Rod Bradley from their Humber Ports Division at Grimsby being seconded to us for several weeks. He told me he didn't see a problem and told me he would check with his Chief Constable and get back to me. Within a quarter of an hour my phone rang. It was Dennis to tell me his Chief Constable had cleared it and, as we spoke, Rod was being asked if he would agree. After a short while Rod rang me to tell me he would be over Monday morning to join us and asked me to sort out accommodation. I told him he would be staying at my house and it would be a pleasure to accommodate him.

When J.R. returned from his aqua sport, I put him in the picture. He was OK with it. He liked Rod and knew where I was coming from by asking BTP for Rod. After all, they were a large part of this operation and had helped so much. Apart from knowing that I could rely on Rod, it would be nice to involve my old force more.

Later that afternoon the Chief Constable came to see us and told us Rod was coming on Monday to assist. Both J.R. and I looked at each other and smiled.

The following Monday, Rod arrived about 10.30 a.m. He came up to the office all suited and booted, looking a little like a Burton's shop dummy, very smart! Anyway, J.R. took him to see the Chief Constable, Mr Donaldson. After ten minutes he emerged, and I took him into the admin office to introduce him to the girls. After all, he would be dealing with them regarding typing etc. I put my mischievous head on and introduced Rod as Chief Superintendent Bradley. Immediately one of the girls asked if he would like a drink of tea. Naturally, the offer was accepted, so I asked if she could make it three, as J.R. would be with us. We went along to the Cabinet office where J.R. was, and after a short time a tray with a pot of tea and biscuits was brought in, very nice it was too. It made a change having tea served in china crockery, rather than mugs. It didn't take long after for word to get to the admin girls that our visitor was Detective Constable Bradley and not of a higher rank. We all had a laugh, even the admin staff.

Rod at that point remembered that he had some fish in the boot for us all. With Grimsby being a fishing port and fresh haddock and cod being landed daily, each time Rod visited us he brought us some fish, which was at wholesale price. So, we quickly brought the boxes of iced fish, which had virtually melted, up to the SOC office, where Ken Tonge, our fingerprint officer, kept his SOCO bags. We raided these, with his consent of course – after all, he was buying fish too. The fish was all bagged up, labelled with names on, and then stored in the canteen fridge. Rod as a side-line also dealt in suit lengths and permanently had a few in his boot, constantly trying to sell one or two. In fact, I think most of the detectives, court officers and solicitors around Humberside were sporting a suit from material supplied by Rod.

The rest of the first day was spent bringing Rod up to speed on how the file was being prepared and what outstanding enquiries needed to be done.

On Friday 27th May we finally got the last proposed file on the train to the DPP London. We had worked all week rushing to get the files ready for despatch on that Friday. Les Evans had prepared the file of exhibits amounting to a hundred and fifty sheets of paper. There was a detailed covering report written by J.R. and a file of statement pages, amounting to 378 pages. Four sets of each were boxed up that Friday morning. Time was closing in on us, as we needed to get the boxes onto the noon train from Lime Street Station to London Euston. We left Police HQ at around 11.35 a.m. I drove with speed and, upon entering Lime Street Station, I drove straight onto Platform 7, where the London train was awaiting departure. I spoke to the guard, leaving him in possession of the boxed files. We had arranged with Dennis Ward at BTP HQ for someone to collect the files and deliver them that same afternoon to the DPP's office.

We saw the train off and J.R. said, "Right, time for a drink." He took us to the Polish Club in Catherine Street. I recall as we arrived and parked up there was a brewery rep in a van outside. The door was opened by Anna and her husband, who upon seeing it was J.R. gave us all hugs and handshakes. We were made most welcome and given a pint each. The brewery rep was fitting a new pump to which he connected a small keg of beer. It was a new trial brand, and I can't remember the name. Anyway, to cut a long story short, by 3.30 p.m. we had drunk it dry and consumed two or three large trays of sandwiches provided by Anna. It was plain to see that the couple thought a lot of J.R. He had been a detective covering their area for years, so he knew them quite well.

Later that month (May) I received another letter from Ken Candler, in which he raised his concern over getting the case committed to the Crown Court. He feared the defendants would seek an Oral Committal. For those of you who are not "AU FAIT" with this term allow me to explain.

A committal hearing is held before Magistrates, who decide if there is sufficient evidence for an accused person to be committed to the Crown Court for trial. If there is no objection from the defendant(s) then the Magistrates will automatically send the case to the Crown court to be dealt with.

At least Fourteen days prior to such a hearing, the defence may request an "Oral Committal". Which means they may request certain or all witnesses to attend and give evidence in order that the Magistrates may then reach a decision, as to there being sufficient evidence to commit the case to the Crown Court.

What Ken was concerned about, had already gone through our minds, should a request be made by the defence, for an "Oral Committal" then we may have had real problems getting the foreign witnesses back, then again, had they attended and the case had been successfully committed , would we be able to secure a second return of witnesses from various parts of the world, to give that evidence a second time in a later trial.

As it transpired an "Oral Committal" was not requested and the case was committed to the Crown Court for trial. I don't know why the defence did not seek such a move; it could well have thrown a spanner in the works. I suspect possibly, the defence Barristers agreed it may look bad on their client having caused witnesses to be brought to the UK twice, if sentencing took place at a later date, if their clients were found guilty, a Judge may take this into consideration and form the opinion that such a move was merely a ploy, to cause problems. Thank goodness this didn't occur.

Nine

D-DAY, 8TH JUNE 1983

D-Day, 8th June 1983

In the weeks previous, J.R. had liaised with a contact of his at Merseyside Police, Detective Chief Inspector Dave Liptrot at the Regional Crime squad. We were obviously going to need assistance, to execute several simultaneous arrests, after all we were only a small force with limited resources.

Arrangements were made and several officers from both the Regional and Serious Crime Squads in Liverpool were to be allocated to assist, together with uniformed officers from the OSD (Operational Support Division).

On 6th June, having typed up seven arrest warrants and ten warrants to search the suspects' home addresses (we added a couple of known addresses just in case we failed to locate the target at his home address), I attended South Sefton Magistrates Court, where the warrants were applied for and suitably endorsed by a Magistrate, thus making them enforceable.

All was going to plan, and the day before the planned raids, Tuesday 7th June, Miss Phillips (DPP's office) arrived in Liverpool by train bringing the Letters of Authority to act. We needed these, as they absolved our force from footing the bill. This was going to be a very costly exercise, estimated at well over £100K should it go to a full trial, taking an estimated eight weeks, which we, the Port of

Liverpool Police, obviously could not afford. I remember that afternoon preparing all the necessary individual files for each team of officers (who would carry out the raids), which included arrest warrants and search warrants together with an up-to date photograph of each suspect. We retired around 4 p.m. to the Club Ship Landfall at Bramley Moor Dock for a few pints and last-minute discussions. Then home we went.

The following morning around 5.15 a.m. we all attended at St Anne's Street Police Station, Liverpool for a pre-raid briefing. I remember seeing Ted Norris and his colleague, Jim Duncan from Lancashire Constabulary, they had slept the night in the lounge there, after availing themselves of the bar facilities the evening before.

All together there were seven teams of officers, totalling well over fifty. Each team consisted of one detective from our force, a detective from the British Transport Police and either three or four Regional or Serious Crime Squad detectives, together with OSD officers. The two Lancashire detectives assisted in one search, as they had an interest in that particular suspect. After J.R. addressed the briefing the teams were handed their respective folders containing the suspects' details, photographs, warrants etc. We all went down to the yard at St Anne's and to our respective crime squad vehicles. Two Regional Crime squad officers accompanied me and Maureen Ross, a colleague. We decided to have policewoman with us, as the suspect we were after, was married with small children and in the event of any problems Maureen could assist. As the convoy of over twenty vehicles pulled out of the yard and onto Great Homer Street, heading towards Bootle and the targets addresses, I recall thinking to myself, this is it, five years of work, how many will we net? I kept checking the observers mirror on route to our suspects address and seeing parts of the convoy peel off, heading to their respective target addresses.

We had arranged to hit the houses simultaneously at 6 a.m. All the suspects bar two were found at their addresses and arrested. Interestingly though, one suspect's bed was apparently still warm! Property was seized, consisting of documents, photographs and other incriminating items.

All the prisoners were transported to various police stations in Liverpool, then later brought to the main Bridwell, Cheapside, Liverpool, where I interviewed them in the presence of Rod Bradley and another colleague. I read out a series of questions to each suspect which Rod had compiled. This process had taken him several days, extracting information from statements we held, covering the incidents appertaining to each individual suspect.

All five suspects refused to answer any questions bar one, **Suspect R,** who did give a couple of replies. These were noted on the contemporaneous question and answer sheet, Rod had prepared.

Later that morning the suspects were transported to Marsh Lane Police Station, Bootle, where the circumstances of their arrests was outlined to the Bridewell Sergeant there before I charged them.

The following morning all five appeared before South Sefton Magistrates Court and were remanded in custody pending appearance at Liverpool Crown Court on a date to be fixed.

In relation to our two outstanding targets, they were subsequently arrested and charged. The first surrendered to Lancashire Constabulary at Heysham the next day, 9th June. Rod, another officer and myself collected him, bringing him back to Liverpool. The other was arrested on 11th August 1983 by a very astute RCS officer, Ted Potter, who spotted him driving in Liverpool. He was followed and a traffic car was used to stop him, thus effecting his arrest. Both men were remanded in custody along with their accomplices awaiting trial at Liverpool Crown Court.

The suspects faced Fourteen charges, which varied amongst them. For example:

Charge 1. Related to ***Suspects P, Q, L, T and D.***

On divers' dates between the 17th August 1979 and 6th February 1980 you did conspire with other persons known and unknown to enter inhabited merchant vessels as trespassers and to steal there from.

Contrary to section 1(1) of the Criminal Law Act 1977.

Charge 4. Related to ***Suspects P, Q, K, and D.***

On divers' dates between 12th June 1980 and the 22nd January 1981 you did conspire together and with persons known and unknown to enter inhabited merchant vessels as trespassers and to steal therefrom.

Contrary to section 1(1) of the Criminal Law Act 1977.

<u>*Charge 5.*</u> *Against* ***Suspect K*** *alone. (This related to an offence committed at Felixstowe Docks).*

On 10th July 1980 having entered an inhabited merchant vessel namely the MV Clerk Maxwell as a trespasser stole therein £20, 4800 Pesetas, 10 Guilders and 183 US dollars in money.

Contrary to Section 9(1) (b) of the Theft Act 1968.

<u>*Charge 6.*</u> *Against* ***Suspect Q*** *alone. (This related to an offence committed at Immingham docks.)*

On the 10th September 1980, having entered an inhabited merchant vessel namely the MV Esperanza stole a safe and the contents including £2500, 30.000 Drachma in money and a semi-automatic pistol and ammunition.

Contrary to Section 9 (1) (b) of the Theft Act 1968.

<u>*Charge 8*</u>*. Against* ***Suspects P, L and R.***

On divers' dates between the 25th September 1981 and the 27th April 1982 conspired together and with other persons known and unknown to enter inhabited merchant vessels as trespassers and to steal therefrom.

Contrary to Section 1 (1) of the Criminal Law Act 1977.

Charge 9. Against **Suspect R** *alone. (This charge relates to an offence committed at Redcar Docks)*

On 26th September 1981 having entered an inhabited merchant vessel namely the MV Energy Transmission as a trespasser stole 14.800 US Dollars in money.

Contrary to Section 9 (1) (b) of the Theft Act 1968.

Charge 10. Against **Suspects P and R.** *(This incident related to a theft at Holyhead Docks)*

On 28th October 1981 having entered the inhabited merchant vessel MV Claire A Tsavlieris as a trespasser stole therefrom £6000, in money.

Contrary to Section 9 (1) (b) of the Theft Act 1968.

Charge 11. Against **Suspect L** *alone. (This related to an offence committed at Heysham Docks)*

On 25th November 1982 having entered an inhabited merchant vessel namely MV Andra as a trespasser stole therein 23.000 Deutch Marks and 12.581 US Dollars in money.

Contrary to Section 9 (1) (b) of the Theft Act 1968.

Also

Against **Suspects P and K.**

On 27th January 1981 for the purpose of procuring a passport for himself namely a British Visitors Passport number XXXXXX did make a certain statement which was to his knowledge untrue.

Contrary to Section 36 of the Criminal Justice Act 1925.

Suspect T. Was also charged with a likewise offence.

The above are extracts of the fourteen charges drafted by the DPP.

Ten

FURTHER BANK AND FINANCIAL ENQUIRIES

Further Bank and Financial Enquiries

The next week was spent on paperwork, sorting through the evidence found during the searches of the suspects' homes. Les Evans, who was our Exhibits Officer, itemised the exhibits, making a reference sheet. Various paperwork, such as travel documents, receipts showing considerable expenditure etc was found in some houses. One of our lads Alan Ogley had found some photographs at the home of **Suspect K** ,not only would they assist in proving association but one of these showed another suspect(not part of our main players) lying on what appeared to be a hotel bed, stretched out on his back covered in US 100 Dollar bills. We guessed this was probably taken in Amsterdam, on one of the many visits made there.

On Monday 13th June 1983, Rod and I attended at South Sefton Magistrates Court, where we met with Ted Pugh, the Clerk of the Court.

Ted was an old-fashioned clerk. He ran the court his way. You could ask Ted for favours, such as a "remand in custody for three days" in relation to a prisoner (commonly known as a three-day lie down), and as sure as eggs were eggs the Magistrates would retire to consider the prosecution's request (our request). Ted would advise them, and they would emerge and say, "Granted." He really was a great guy and had no time for the toe rags.

We had prepared several Bankers Book Evidence Act Orders. For the benefit of those reading this who are not familiar with the process, let me explain. The order is like a search warrant. The details were entered onto a prescribed form showing details of the bank to be visited, suspect's name and account number, if known, or just enter "to inspect foreign currency transaction slips", followed by the date.

Then we would attend court, go before a magistrate with the Clerk of the Court present, explain why we needed the order and make the application on oath by swearing on the Bible, that the contents of the order and the application was true. The magistrate then granted the order, signing it at the bottom. The next step was to visit the branch of the bank concerned and serve a copy of the order upon the manager. This then meant that we would return after three clear days, which gave him time to locate the documents for us to inspect. So, this is what we did on that morning, both Rod and I taking out several orders, then visiting the banks concerned, serving the orders upon the managers and arranging follow-up appointments to inspect the records.

On the Thursday and Friday that week we visited two banks in Liverpool, where we inspected their records. The banks were extremely helpful. They provided a room for us to work in, and we even got a brew. There were more visits in the following weeks, and in between we obtained a few more orders, serving them on the respective banks. This process was repeated for weeks, creating about four or five visits per week, obtaining the evidence, bringing it back to the office, entering it into the system and so on. We were kept busy throughout June, July and into August. I think

Rod had one week's leave during this time. It was non-stop. As for myself, I decided not to take any leave that summer, my wife and I had nothing planned anyway, it was nose to the grindstone.

Out of the numerous banks visited throughout Merseyside, one was in the New Strand, Bootle. On our initial visit there whilst serving the Bankers Book Evidence Act Order upon the manager, he had commented that as far as he was concerned, he was not going to assist us, and in fact he would not be doing so, as in his (infinite wisdom) opinion, foreign currency exchange slips did not come under the terms of the Bankers Book Evidence Act order. I told him straight, that I would be back at the prescribed time and date, which I notified him of and left.

The next morning Rod and I visited the courts in Bootle to obtain a couple more orders. I mentioned to Ted Pugh, the Clerk, that this particular bank manager was not prepared to comply with the order we had served upon him. I could clearly see the change in Ted's face. He said, "When you return, if he doesn't comply, arrest him for obstruction and bring him straight here to go before the court."

Two days later, Rod and I attended at the given time, at the bank. The manager was still adamant he was not prepared to allow us access to the foreign exchange slips. I told him that in that case I would have to arrest him for obstructing me in the execution of my duty. He paused and beckoned us into a side office, saying he was going to ring the bank's security department in London. I agreed, and he rang the number in our presence. He outlined his objections to the person at the other end, who must have asked to speak to me. The manager then handed me the phone saying, "Will you please speak to our Mr `B`, I agreed and said, "Hello Les," for I knew Les the security manager from other enquiries I had been conducting. He was ex-job and liked to help the police as much as he was permitted to do. I saw the expression on the manager's face change as I explained the situation. Les asked to speak to the manager again, which he did. The one side of the conversation we could hear went like this: "Yes Mr Bartlett, no Mr. Bartlett, yes Mr Bartlett." I was then handed the phone. Les said, "I've just told that idiot to comply, unless he wants to be arrested." We had no problem after the call ended and inspected the documentation, taking what evidence we needed.

The months of July, August and into September were spent visiting banks and building societies, searching records, locating transactions, making appointments and following up with visits to obtain witness statements. In between we entered our findings onto a manual spreadsheet (remember, no computers back then). This showed the date of the transaction, type of currency, amount, Bank of England equivalent of value, bank where exchanged and by whom if known, etc.

In between all the above, other enquiries were being made, and J.R. was getting to grips with the instructions in Brian Leveson's advice, which amounted to several pages.

We did manage a break away from all this. BTP Humber Ports Division at Hull hosted a further conference on 19th October 1983. Numerous forces attended, J.R. updated the situation with regards to the DPP file, firstly introducing Eleanor Phillips from the D.P.P.s office who had travelled over to Hull with us the evening before. Tony spoke about the information and publication of bulletins. I gave a slide presentation on the enquiries we had made regarding the exchange of foreign currency at banks in Liverpool, showing copies of transaction slips and how suspects details appeared on those slips, together with signatures. These also showed in some instances that the transaction coincided with a recent theft. Our Dutch colleagues who attended addressed the conference, first Fred Bakker from Amsterdam re sightings and intelligence gatherings, then Eef Krabbendam from Rotterdam on thefts which had occurred in Holland since the last conference and intelligence gathered. The Dutch had a great system regarding the records of hotel guests. They were able to locate suspects staying in Amsterdam quickly, which helped a lot.

It became apparent that the Belgian police, although suffering numerous offences in their ports, clearly had either given up the ghost or were just not interested in joining in this concerted effort to bring these men to justice. They failed to attend and had not contributed in any way of late.

We then discussed the team's movements in France, Sweden and Germany. It was agreed to keep a crossflow of intelligence going regarding other countries, with assistance from Interpol.

Before the end of the conference, J.R. as was his norm, read out a few lines he had composed, which as you will appreciate, made reference to himself and myself. Here it is.

OPERATION CABINET

You will recall how in St. Paul, Chapter 15, verse 7, the disciples went amidst their flocks and gathered unto themselves many writings which they then took to the tabernacle and showed the writings to the Lord, who is known as the D.P.P.

Chapter 16 verse 23 goes onto say,

And the Lord (the D.P.P.) read the writings given unto him and speaketh to St. Paul and St John, saying unto them,

"You have gathered many scriptures and much evil has been done by those itinerant sinners who travel the land and to other shores and stealeth from those who go down to the sea".

I therefore say unto ye, prepare all these things with my blessing, but now you must rest and dine at my table- which meant having a sandwich and a pint at the pub near Queen Anne's Gate, London.

And the next day St. Paul rose again. And on the road to Domestos he met Mary Madelene (I think that was her name)- who said unto St. Paul, you are weary and you must rest and taketh thee another day in lieuth and she bathed his feet- so he says.

And again, the next day and the next day, St. Paul travelled to many places like Gomorrah and Nazareth, (known today as Hull and Immingham) preaching the gospel and the word of the Lord, the D.P.P.

Then on the 8th day- 8th June- the disciples gathered unto themselves and setting out, laid hands on Five of the sinners and cast them into darkness, saying unto them.

"You will doeth" and the next day the disciples set out again and laid hands on another and said unto him also, "you too will doeth" and later, having rested from their labours laid hands on yet another, making seven, saying unto all of them, "Repenteth thee, your time draweth nigh".

And it came to pass that when the learned apostles - known as the Chief Constable and other senior officers - read the scriptures that had been gathered by St. Paul, they shook their heads and whispered amongst themselves saying, "We thinketh not it could be done" and St. Paul, cried " Oh ye of little faith", behold these sinners and woe not, for on the 4th day of Michaelmas – which for those who know not is from the 1st day of October to the 21st December - on the 4th day of Michaelmas the sinners were taken from where they had been cast and delivered unto the Chief Magistrate – known as committal proceedings hence, have been called to judgement at the next sitting of the Crown court, and low and behold, the Apostles -The Chief Constable- smiled down on St. Paul- not a lot- and on the 18th, a multitude of Disciples gathered unto themselves at the tabernacle in Gomorrah (Hull) where they praised the Lord exceedingly and rejoiced and drank wine.

Amen

The conference then came to an end.

We knew of over 850 thefts from ships' cabins that had been reported since 1976, with over £734,000 in currencies being stolen. This did not include any details of thefts from Belgium, France, Germany and other countries. In all, it was estimated that thefts had well exceeded the magic million pounds (quite an amount in those days and near to Four

Million Pounds at today's value). Now I must add here that we obviously could not categorically prove our team of suspects, who were over twenty strong, were responsible for every single offence but we estimated they were responsible for a lot.

Over the years we had some success apprehending members of the team, either in possession of foreign currency or, in fact, attempting to exchange it at a bank.

For instance, in September 1981, a theft had occurred involving a large amount of US dollars. We alerted banks in Liverpool, and on Monday 28th September 1981 two of our suspects presented themselves at Barclays International Bank, Water Street, Liverpool and requested to exchange 1,000 US dollars.

The cashier was aware of our interest in anyone attempting to exchange such a large amount of dollars and asked her colleague to summon the police. She meanwhile stalled the suspect, counting the notes twice, thus giving time for the local police to attend and both men were arrested. Although the money could not be directly linked to the theft, it was seized. Both suspects were later released.

On 25th November 1982 (the very same day we were all attending a conference in Hull), a theft of 24,260 deutschmarks (no Euros then) and 12,581 US dollars took place onboard the *M.V. Andrea* berthed at the Port of Heysham, Lancashire. The theft was discovered by the Captain after doing his rounds. He had failed to lock his cabin door and upon return to his cabin saw the safe keys lying on his desk. They had been left in a drawer under an envelope.

The second mate had earlier confronted a stranger onboard who he thought was a dockside official.

On 1st December, as a result of us alerting banks in Liverpool that large amounts of German and American currency might be presented for exchange, Lloyds Bank in Water Street, Liverpool, rang for police assistance. One of our suspects had attempted to exchange 4,000 US dollars, which as you will now have realised is more or less a third share of the dollars stolen the week previous.

The subject was arrested and charged with theft at Heysham. This charge was later added to the list of charges against the suspect, as a substantive charge, listed amongst other charges in our operation.

When the suspects' houses were searched following the raids, officers took possession of quite a few receipts for cash purchases of furniture and other goods. These amounts in some instances were quite sizeable payments, and this obviously helped us prove that their expenditure well exceeded their official income.

Of course, all these transactions at the bank and cash purchases needed to be shown in additional evidence, so we set about compiling a chart regarding the currency exchange incidents.

FOREIGN CURRENCY BANK TRANSACTIONS

All the foreign currency transaction slips that we found in the banks, which we took possession of, and I have listed within these pages, bore the names and addresses of our suspects. They had also been signed in the suspect's respective name. This meant that either our suspects themselves exchanged the currency or a third party carried out the transaction using the particular suspects details. We must remember that more than likely, the cashier in the bank would have asked for some form of identification.

("Oh, what a Tangled Web We Weave, When First We Practice to Deceive", Sir Walter Scott 1808)

Although I have covered the subject of enquiries at banks, I am including a few instances concerning enquiries re foreign currency cash transactions here, as these took place during 1981/82 and give an insight into the complexity of the investigations undertaken.

When we looked into the foreign cash transactions at banks in Merseyside, we discovered evidence that indicated the following transactions had taken place.

On 23rd April 1982 "**Suspect P**" exchanged 4,000 US dollars and received £2,221.22. He entered his correct name and home address on the exchange slip he completed at the time in the bank.

On 24th April 1982 at Lloyds Bank, Liverpool, **Suspect P** exchanged 12,180 US dollars and was paid £6,682.13 by the cashier. **Suspect P**, then opened a bank account with £4,682.13. The remaining £2000 he kept.

On 30th April 1981 **Suspect P**, using a false name and address, exchanged 3,236 US dollars and was paid £1,473.26. The home address given was in fact that of another suspect.

Further digging into records showed a person who we suspected at the time was **Suspect P** using the same false name and address, exchanging 3,800 US dollars ***on 2nd June 1981,*** and receiving the sum of £1,804.23.

Interestingly here, the false name used, was the same name the suspect had used when purchasing a property. Enquiries with the vendor of that property showed the suspect paid £5,000 with a building society cheque for furnishings and fittings. When that line of enquiry was pursued, we discovered the account was held by a female with the same surname as the false name previously given. The account at one time had held over £20,000.

Further enquiries at the building society showed that a person, believed to be the sister-in-law of **Suspect P** held an account which had been opened on ***4th March 1981*** with a deposit of £10,783.75, some of it paid in by cash and some by a cheque issued by a Liverpool solicitor. It transpired the solicitor's cheque was the proceeds from the sale of a house owned by **Suspect P**.

On 10th March 1981, **Suspect P** purchased his previous house using a building society cheque. This account was opened on ***3rd October 1979*** with a deposit of a few hundred pounds. Further enquiries showed that on the same day another person (**Suspect T**) opened an account at the same building society branch. That suspect, when eventually closing that account, cleared his cheque via a bank account. Enquiries at that bank showed his wife had held four accounts at that branch, some of which had held or been opened with several thousands of pounds.

At the same time, we discovered that a further suspect (**Suspect L**) had held an account at the same branch, using the address of **Suspect T**.

On 4th November 1982, **Suspect P** then exchanged 10,700 US dollars, for which he received £6,310.

During enquiries we discovered that another suspect (**Suspect Q**) had held an account at a bank, in Bootle. ***On 13th March 1981,*** a credit of £3,107.39 was made to that account. This was linked to a bank in Liverpool. Enquiries there showed that on 11th March a foreign currency exchange had been carried out bearing the details of **Suspect L**, who had exchanged 7,260 US dollars, receiving £3,207.39. It appeared **Suspect L** had kept £100 (spending money) and transferred £3,107.39 to the account of **Suspect Q.** A similar transaction took place on 2nd April 1981, when 4,650 US dollars and 235,000 Japanese yen were exchanged, and the funds were again paid into the account of **Suspect Q**

Numerous other transactions were traced, but I hope the above gives you, the reader, an insight into the complexity of the enquiries undertaken during this operation.

OTHER BANK TRANSACTIONS

BETWEEN JUNE 1980 AND DECEMBER 1982

Again, details of our suspects were found on transaction slips as follows, together with signatures, the same scenario would apply here, either the suspect themselves entered their details or a third party carried out the transaction using the suspects details.

On 13.6.80 **D** exchanged 1,081 US Dollars for £452.37p, at Lloyds Bank Building, Liverpool.

On 18.6.80 **P** (using the name Another) exchanged 300 US Dollars and 4,110 Dutch Guilders at Lloyds Bank, India Buildings, Liverpool for £1,003.46p.

On 27.10.80 **K** exchanged 620 US Dollars for £247.01 at the Midland Bank, Bootle.

On 4.11.80 **Q** exchanged 1,000 Deutschmarks and 500 US Dollars for £403.50p at National Westminster Bank, Bootle.

On 17.11.80 **D** exchanged 1,000 US Dollars for £405.69p at Lloyds Bank, India Building, Liverpool.

On 19.11.80 **K** exchanged 23,000 Japanese Yen, 60,000 Lire, 100 Deutschmarks and 50 Greek

Drachma for £91.00 at the Midland Bank, Bootle.

On 21.11.80 **D** exchanged 468 Dollars for £192.00 at National Westminster Bank, Bootle.

On 24.11.80 **Q** exchanged 60,000 Japanese Yen, 100 Deutschmarks, 469 US Dollars for £325.65 at Barclays Bank, Bootle.

On 15.12.80 **P** (using the name Another) exchanged 200,000 Japanese Yen and 1,200 US Dollars for £899.83p at Lloyds Bank, India Buildings, Liverpool.

On 9.2.81 **L** exchanged 360 US Dollars for £150.60p at the Midland Bank, Castle Street, Liverpool, and the same day he exchanged (in the name of Another) 320 Dollars for £130.58p at Williams & Glynns Bank, Dale Street, Liverpool.

On 3.3.81 **L** exchanged 200 Deutschmarks and 95 Dutch Guilders for £57.47p at Williams & Glynns Bank, Dale Street, Liverpool.

On 3.3.81 **L** (in the name of Another) exchanged 450 US Dollars and 160 Deutchmarks for £233.98 at Lloyds Bank, India Building, Liverpool.

On 3.3.81	**D** exchanged 5,200 US Dollars for £2,330.84p at Lloyds Bank, India Building, Liverpool.
On 11.3.81	**K** exchanged 7,520 US Dollars, for £3,326.43p at Lloyds Bank, India Buildings, Liverpool.
On 13.3.81	**K** exchanged 1200 US Dollars for £527.65 at National Westminster Bank, Bootle.
On 11.3.81	**K** exchanged 7,260 US Dollars for £3,207.39 at Midland Bank, Dale Street.
On 13.3.81	**Q & K** £3,107.39 was paid into the account of **Q** at National Westminster, Bootle, where reference was made to the above transaction by **K.**
On 2.4.81	**Q** exchanged 4,650 US Dollars and 242,000 Japanese Yen for £2,535.35p at Lloyds Bank, India Buildings.
On 2.4.81	**Q** exchanged 325 Dutch Guilders and 130 US Dollars for £116.36p at Lloyds Bank, India Buildings.
On 2.4.81	**Q** exchanged 4,650 US Dollars and 235,000 Japanese Yen for £2,511.66p at Barclays International Bank, Castle Street, Liverpool. (This money was paid into his account at National Westminster Bank, Bootle on 13.4.81).

On 1.6.81	**Q** exchanged 2,470 Dutch Guilders and 220 US Dollars for £548.34p at the National Westminster Bank, Bootle.
On 1.6.81	**K** exchanged 900 US Dollars for £422.14 at Lloyds Bank, India Buildings, Liverpool.
On 2.6.81	**P** (using the name Another) exchanged 3,800 US Dollars for £1,804.23p at Lloyds Bank, India Buildings.
On 9.6.81	**Q** exchanged 400 US Dollars for £200.10p at the National Westminster Bank, Bootle.
On 24.6.81	**K** exchanged 1,000 Greek drachma and 300 US Dollars for £153.62 at the National Westminster Bank, Bootle.
On 26.6.81	**K** exchanged 1,100 US Dollars for £544.15p at Lloyds Bank, India Buildings, Liverpool, this transaction also bears the name of **Suspect Q**.
On 19.10.81	**Q** exchanged 39,000 Greek drachma for £316.77p at Midland Bank, Castle Street, Liverpool.
On 19.10.81	**Q** exchanged 31,000 Greek drachma for £253.69p at the National Westminster Bank, Victoria Street, Liverpool.

On 19.10.81	**Q** exchanged 26,000 Greek drachma, 1,135 US Dollars and 60 Venezuelan dollars for (£851.00 at Lloyds Bank, India Buildings, Liverpool.
On 18.3.82	**K** exchanged 300 US Dollars for £160.14p at Midland Bank, Bootle.
On 18.3.82	(A separate transaction) **K** exchanged 18,150 Hong Kong Dollars for £1,695.50p at Midland Bank, Bootle.
On 25.3.82	**K** exchanged 13,320 US Dollars for £7,288.63 at Midland Bank, Bootle.
On 16.7.82	**R** exchanged 200 US Dollars for £112.18p at Midland Bank, Bootle.
On 16.7.82	**R** exchanged 1,000 Portuguese escudos for £6.30p at the Midland Bank, Bootle.
On 11.10.82	**Q** exchanged 705. US Dollars for £397.81 at Lloyds Bank, India Buildings, Liverpool.
On 22.10.82	**Q** exchanged 1,685 US Dollars for £961.86p at Lloyds Bank, India Buildings, Liverpool.
On 20.12.82	**Q** exchanged 170 US Dollars for £102.22 at the National Westminster Bank, Bootle.

On 24.12.82 **Q** exchanged 40 Canadian Dollars for £18.92p at the National Westminster Bank, Bootle.

The respective total amounts of foreign currency exchanges **discovered in the names of our suspects** by December 1982 were as follows: -

P	£22,703.57
K	£21,251.35
D	£ 5,473.49
L	£ 615.11
Q	£10,213.47
R	£ 435.22
T	£ 12.27

During the course of visiting banks, we discovered one particular transaction that took place at the Nat. West. Bank, Bootle, where on 6th August 1979, 1269 U.S. Dollars were exchanged, and the transaction slip showed the details of one of our main suspect's wives. The suspect himself at that time was on remand in custody in Antwerp, Belgium. Antwerp of course is one of the world's major shipping ports.

I decided not to pursue any enquiries in relation to this transaction, as we had obviously located more than enough evidence against our subject and what would we achieve after all, the arrest of a wife who would probably have come up with a plausible excuse anyway, plus the fact I suppose she needed to provide for her children.

Eleven

COURT DATES AND WITNESSES

Court Dates and Witnesses

With all the suspects now held on remand in custody, we were under pressure to have the additional evidence, prepared and served upon the defence. The actual trial itself had been set to commence on Monday 23rd January 1984 at the Old Session House, Liverpool before Judge Lawton.

On Christmas Eve morning 1983 we received a call from Brian Leveson requesting someone visit his Junior Barrister's home address in Liverpool. Later that afternoon I attended, where I met Mr Smith and was shown into in an empty upstairs bedroom, strewn all over the floor, was a copy of our file, which had been taken apart.

The final file contained 378 statement pages of evidence.

The exhibit file contained 187 pages of paper exhibits.

There were also 37 disclosure statements, some several pages in length, these were statements that had been obtained during the course of the investigation but were not included in the evidence being submitted against the accused. None the less they had to be made available to the defence, in order to show we were not holding anything back.

We both sat on the floor attempting to make sense of some confusion that had arisen over certain points in the file. I remember thinking at the time, "I really don't want to be doing this." It was Christmas Eve, I wanted to get home. Fortunately, the problem was sorted fairly quickly, and after an hour or so, I was away.

Two Pre-Trial Reviews were to take place, one on 2nd December 1983 and a further was due to take place on 3rd January 1984.

Despite those Pre-Trial Reviews, on 18th January, one of the accused lodged an appeal of "Autrefois Acquit" in relation to part of the evidence now submitted, which referred to a previous arrest, court appearance and the eventual offering of no evidence by the prosecution in respect of that incident. The very next day, another of the accused again lodged a similar appeal. Basically, what the defence were saying was, it would be wrong to include as part of the evidence, a set of circumstances regarding an incident that the defendant had already appeared before the court on and had been discharged from.

In other words, the defendant had been arrested some time previously for an offence but as the witnesses were not available (the ship had sailed) the case against him had been withdrawn and it was felt, that it was wrong to include that specific evidence, in the evidence we were presenting.

Following discussions, with the prosecution counsels Mr Leveson and Mr Smith, together with Judge Mr Lawton and defence counsel in the Judge's chambers, both appeals were subsequently withdrawn before the court.

Throughout December 1983 and early January 1984, I had been heavily engaged in contacting witnesses who would be required to attend court and give evidence in the event of not guilty pleas and a trial going ahead. This was quite a mammoth task. I had nearly all the witnesses' full details, home addresses and some home telephone contact details.

I First of all, contacted the shipping agents at the ports where the vessel was registered. So, for example, in the case of witnesses from the *Giannis N*, a Greek ship registered in Piraeus, Greece, first of all I rang the shipping agent in Greece, advised him which witness was required to attend court in Liverpool and on what date. I would ask the witness to be informed as soon as possible, adding that a flight would be booked to Manchester in the UK and arrangements would be made for flight tickets to be collected from the airport they were departing from. Contact details, where notifications could be sent to, were obtained.

This was followed up by a teleprinter message to that contact (remember, no fax or emails in those days) confirming the conversation which had just taken place and requesting a reply of confirmation. I then sent the same request to Interpol London, asking for them to notify Interpol Athens to alert the witness direct, who of course in both instances might at that time be at sea anywhere in the world. It seemed to work well, but I knew from experience not to rely on Interpol too much. Interpol London was great. They did their job well. However, when it came to the request being administered abroad, well, it was a bit mañana, if you get my drift. Personally speaking, as far as I was concerned the Interpol request was just to back things up, so if there was a no-show of a particular witness, I could prove I had tried my utmost to ensure we got the witness to court.

As far as arranging flights was concerned, I arranged these through a Manchester-based company I knew who were more than helpful, well they should have been, my cousin Bill, owned it, this meant we were able to cancel the bookings at short notice, if needed.

Accommodation was arranged at two hotels out of the city, and several rooms were pre-booked just in case.

All went well, prior to the trial date. Initial witnesses were lined up and received their flight notifications and tickets etc.

Rod had arranged for interpreters to be on standby if needed.

I remember attempting to contact a witness, a ship's Captain who lived in Korea (Interpol could not assist, as Korea were not members). Having obtained, via the Foreign Office, a contact telephone number for the police in Korea, I set about attempting to make contact. I had no shipping agent details. It was going to have to be a case of making contact directly and trying to get the witness to liaise via a Korean shipping agent or the British Embassy or consulate there.

Having made a call to the telephone number I had been given, the person answering, spoke good English. I explained my problem and furnished him with the details of the witness, name and home address etc. I was then told the witness lived in a more remote part of Korea, so I would be put through to Sector Fifteen Police Station. That was when, everything went pear-shaped. My transferred call to Sector Fifteen was answered by someone who obviously did not speak a word of English, pidgin or otherwise. So, there was I, trying to speak to this person in very slow pidgin English, apparently going red at the gills and waving my arms around. I think you can imagine the scene. Both Rod and J.R. thought it was hilarious. I gave up in the end, and we all had a good laugh.

The enquiry was followed up via the Foreign Office.

I recall one afternoon Les Evans and myself were attempting to warn a witness, who lived in Seattle, USA, we rang, the Seattle Police Dept, to ask them to send a car around to the witness's address, in order to ascertain where he was and his availability for court. My phone call was answered by a female, who introduced herself as, "complaint taker Stacey". By the accent and tone of voice, I had a vision of a blonde middle-aged female, sat there chewing on her gum and doing her nails until the next call came in. Following the usual introductions and me explaining the nature of my call, I was interrupted by Les, who was listening in, He Said, "ask her what she looks like". I swiftly told him to shut up and carried on with our conversation. When the call ended, we had a good laugh.

On the weekend of 21st/22nd January the initial witnesses had flown into Manchester and were met upon arrival and looked after by one of our officers, housing them in their hotel accommodation.

On Sunday 22nd January various colleagues met up, Fred Bakker from Amsterdam, had flown in, Rod came over from Grimsby and Bob Wilson, a D.S. from Port of Bristol Police, arrived.

Ken Candler had flown back from Hong Kong, and it was good to see him. On the Sunday evening we all met at up at the Montrose Pub, Duke Street, Liverpool. This had become another of our sub-offices, thanks to J.R. It was run by a Chinese gentleman called Ernie Woo, what a character. He had run a couple of clubs in Liverpool, and that's how J.R. had come to know him. He really looked after us and treated us to his special barbecued ribs, his house speciality, which went down well with a few pints. Ernie loved to boast that his chef had worked for the Queen at Buckingham Palace, true or false I will never know, but one thing was for sure, the ribs were to die for, what a sauce. We all caught up with past events, discussing recent developments and then retired for the evening.

It seemed a pity that Ken, hadn't been there to see the investigation through and been involved in the preparation of the file. He had left for Hong Kong prior to us really getting to grips with the task in hand.

Twelve

THE TIME OF RECKONING

The Time of Reckoning

On the morning of Monday 23rd January 1984, J.R, Rod, Les Evans, our Exhibits officer and myself, left the office around 9.10 a.m. for the Crown Court, at Liverpool. The trial was to be held in the Old Sessions House, next to St. Georges Hall.

Upon arrival we met with Brian Leveson and his junior, Mr Smith. A quick discussion took place, and then the first three Greek witnesses were brought into the courthouse and placed in the witness room, where an officer looked after them.

Later that morning the usual formalities took place – discussions between prosecution counsel and counsel for the defendants, which amounted to fourteen barristers in all, each defendant having a lead and junior barrister.

It was not until Tuesday afternoon that we got into court before the judge and legal submissions and arguments took place. This procedure took three days, then finally on the Thursday the jury were sworn in and opening speeches made.

During the course of that week, Tony Wrench, who I have previously mention as being very artistic, had taken up Glass Engraving, He purchased a few glass tankards, firstly engraving the Operation Cabinet Motif, that myself and Mike Trewhella had designed, onto one side of each glass. Then all of us applied our signature on a piece of paper. This was then inserted inside the glass, held in place so the signature was visible on the outside. Tony then engraved over the signature. The end result, being we, all had a glass which bore everyone's signature, as a Memento of the operation.

On the Friday morning the defence had a lengthy conference with the judge in chambers. Shortly prior to lunch we were informed that some plea bargaining had taken place, and all the defendants were prepared to enter guilty pleas to certain charges. The respective charges were then put to each defendant, who entered a guilty plea.

The charges which had been drawn up by the DPP covered *inter alia* several charges of conspiracy to steal from ships' cabins on divers' dates (various different defendants in each case), several independent substantive charges of burglary and, against three of the defendants, charges of obtaining false British Visitor Passports.

Defence counsel made their submissions, the lead barrister, Mr Cunningham, saying:

> *"It should be said that the preparation of this case is one which will invite tribute from your Honour to the officers concerned and the officer in charge of this case, and Mr Leveson should also be noted. He has been most helpful in the final approach to these proceedings, through which it became easier for advice to be given and for my client to accept that advice, and your*

Honour will give him full consideration that not a single witness was required to be brought ... Learned Counsel has not yet worked out the amounts, either in drachma or yen, which have been saved."

Judge Lawton then adjourned and stated that sentencing would take place after lunch.

In the afternoon Judge Lawton sentenced the defendants as follows.

Two defendants (**P and L**) were sentenced to five years' imprisonment, and the others received varying sentences of between six- and eighteen-months' imprisonment.

Following sentencing and the prisoners being taken to the cells below, I was called into the witness box. Judge Lawton praised the prosecution for the exceptional presentation of the file of evidence, addressing the court as follows:

"I have one very pleasant duty, Mr Leveson, and that is this: all the officers in this case have obviously worked extremely hard, and they are all to be commended and congratulated. I know those who have taken the lesser part will understand when I say that, and I think, having read the papers, and as you know, I have had them in my possession for many months now, it seems to me that briefly I should single out Mr Ralphson, Detective Chief Inspector, who is co-ordinating and in charge of this, Detective Constable Evans, Detective Sergeant Wrench and the now retired Detective Sergeant Candler of the Port of Liverpool Police, and Detective Constable Bradley of

Humberside, and last but certainly no means least, Mr Kenyon himself. I realise the very hard and valuable work he has put in."

Mr Leveson replied:

"Your Honour, had he been giving evidence in a trial he would been giving evidence many times and has been responsible for drawing up all the schedules."

His Hon. Judge Lawton:

"Yes. I hope the services of those officers, Kenyon in particular, will be drawn to the authorities."

Mr Leveson:

"I will ensure that is done."

COPY OF NOTES FROM COURT SHORTHAND WRITER

After the Judge had risen and retired to his chambers, Brian Leveson took me to see him, where I presented both him and Judge Lawton with an Operation Cabinet tie.

It was time for a drink. The Chief Constable, Bill Donaldson, had been in court for the sentencing and had indicated to J.R. that he would treat us to a drink, for all the hard work done.

It was 3.30 p.m., and in those days closing time had officially passed. J.R. told me to get down to Ernie Woo's at the Montrose and pave the way. Rod, Les and I shot off ahead.

Upon arrival the doors were locked, but the lights were on. I climbed up to a window and could see the bar was full. Managing to get Ernie's attention, telling him J.R. and the Chief were on their way. He opened the door, let us in, then shouted in a loud voice, "QUICK, EVERYBODY FUCKY OFFY INTO THE LOUNGE, BIG CHIEF COPPER COMING."

J.R. and the Chief arrived a short while later, and true to his word, he bought us all a couple of rounds of drinks.

After returning to the office and JR cracking a bottle, we wound down and went home for the weekend.

Since the inception of the operation, numerous people had commented, saying we would never get such a case off the ground, never get it through committal, never get the witnesses back for court, let alone obtain convictions.

At the end of the operation JR being JR, produced a sketch headed, QUOTATIONS. (see figure 5)

Figure 5.

QUOTATIONS.
'THEY'LL NEVER GET IT OFF THE GROUND'.
OP CABINET
'THEY'LL NEVER GET IT THROUGH COMMITTAL.'
COMMITTAL
OP CABINET
WITNESSES.
"THEY'LL NEVER GET THEM HERE."
GREECE
HONG KONG
BRAZIL
HOLLAND

L to R

P.C. Ken Balmer explosives and firearms, D.C. Alan Ogley, D.C. Wilf Elliot (Birkenhead) Det.Sgt. Tony Wrench, D.C. Jack Holt centre, A.D.C. Steve Mc Donald, D.C. Mike Hughes, the author, Hilary Whittick Admin, P.C. Kevin Barry, Supt. Bob Physic, Det.Sgt. Peter Heyes, D.C. Les Evans and D.C. Harry McCauley C.I.D. Admin. Seated, *D.C. Jock Meek, D.C. Alex Welford Firearms and Explosives, and Ken Candler.*
Apologies for the three missing Ladies names.

L to R

Det.Sgt. Ron Dix, D.C.I. Dave Liptrot Regional Crime Squad, D.C. Alan Ogley (R.I.P.) ,Hilary Whittick Admin, D.C. Colin Smith(R.I.P.) Det.Sgt. Tony Wrench, Miss Eleanor Phillips D.P.P.s office, the author, Det.Ch.Insp. John Ralphson Det.Sgt. Ted Norris Lancashire Constabulary, Rod Bradley, Seated. Acting Dep.Ch.Constable Tony Weston and Det.Insp.Cliff Hardcastle British Transport Police.

John Ralphson, when a Detective Sergeant in the 1960s
By kind permission of Roland Hatton

Liverpool Port News article, February 1984, courtesy of Mersey Dock and Harbour Company (Peel Management).

• The successful police team: left to right – Detective Chief Inspector John Ralphson, Detective Sergeant Tony Wrench, Chief Constable Bill Donaldson, Detective Constable Les Evans and Detective Constable Paul Kenyon.

How the pirates became landlocked

THE investigations that brought justice for the thousands of wronged mariners took five long years of painstaking work and effort on the part of the Port of Liverpool police.

It all began in earnest early in 1977 when Detective Constable Paul Kenyon spotted links in the wave of crime hitting the docksides and suggested a conference of police from several of the main target ports in the UK.

As the raids increased and widened to ports across the country, then into Europe and further afield the co-incidence in the manner of the thefts became more apparent.

Occasionally someone was caught sneaking around the decks of ships or 'acting as a look out'. But charges were rarely supported as witnesses would have sailed along with the scene of the crime long before those in custody could be brought for trial.

After the launch of 'Operation Cabinet', five years of swapping reports of thefts and descriptions of men arrested or spotted loitering were laboriously checked against foreign currency change records at numerous Merseyside banks and the constant watching, noting and waiting eventually led to the unprecedented trial.

Soon the net was closing in and 'Cabinet' had the co-operation of more than forty different police forces around the world.

The key men in the operation were the Port Police squad in Liverpool who collated the information from all over the world and masterminded the plan to catch the cabin pirates.

Said Detective Constable Paul Kenyon: "The gang realised how easy it was to steal a few quid from unattended cabins of ordinary seamen to those of officers and ships' masters.

DEVOTION

Added John Ralphson, the man who led the squad: "Operation Cabinet has been the main occupation of this office for the last five years and it has taken a great deal of concentration, hard work, long hours and devotion to duty involving a lot of our officers putting in many hours of their own time.

"Our success has been due to the willingness, determination and team spirit that has been the hallmark of this job."

Now a decision on whether to charge the remaining suspects rests with the Director of Public Prosecutions.

Next month: The Port Police . . . the role they play

Eef Krabbendam, courtesy of Eef Krabbendam

Tony Wrench centre left, presents an Operation Cabinet glass engraved tankard to John Ralphson.
Looking on left to right
Ken Candler, Rod Bradley, the author, Jackie Yeu, official Chinese interpreter and Fred Bakker.

Thirteen

CONCLUSION

Conclusion

The following week we were busy writing letters of appreciation to various witnesses, both civilian and police, who had assisted us in our enquiries. Rod had a week off and came back a week later to assist in sorting and filing documents and basically putting the office into mothballs, should we need to resurrect the operation again.

J.R. meanwhile locked himself away in his own office, we later discovered, this was when he wrote a report to the Chief Constable, recommending Merit Awards be given to the team of investigative officers.

We were all furnished with a copy of that report, following receipt of our Merit Awards.

I now include a copy of that report:

For the record it must be said the investigations concerning Operation Cabinet have probably been the most protracted, widespread and far reaching in terms of the period of time covered in the Conspiracies and in terms of involvement with so many Police Forces throughout the United Kingdom, the Continent and even further afield, on record.

It is right too, I believe, to record that whilst the contributions by and liaison and co-operation with other Forces has been first class and much appreciated, the very creditable success of the whole operation including the convictions of the seven principal and determined thieves with the consequential reduction of this class of offence throughout the United Kingdom and the Continental Ports, is due mainly to combined and strenuous efforts of both the Uniformed and Criminal Investigation branches of the Port of Liverpool Police, to which was lent throughout, the full support of the Senior Officers of the Force and Police Authority.

I also believe it would be remiss not to mention the excellent work performed by Mrs Paulette Mitchell the typist, in the preparation of the case papers.

The criminal and suspected activities of the offenders, the wide range of their activities, the complexities of evidence and various procedures created many problems, some of which are enumerated below.

1. *Collation and dissemination of statements of evidence of over 170 witnesses from 17 Police Forces, including foreign witnesses and the question of interpreters.*
2. *Scottish procedures in respect of statements submitted in English courts.*
3. *The effect of the CJA Act 1967 sec.219 and M.C. Rules 1968 & 58 and statements from foreign witnesses made whilst abroad.*
4. *The consideration of Commission Regatoir as it affects certain continental countries and the procedure.*
5. *The problems of obtaining evidence from some 30 Banks, under the provisions of the Bankers Books Evidence Act 1879, s.7.*

6. *The involvement of solicitors representing Building Societies with whom some accused held accounts/ or transacted house purchase on mortgage or alternative.*
7. *Warrants to arrest and search and the consequential effects of the execution of those warrants.*
8. *Complaints possibly resulting from that Police action.*
9. *Previous convictions – admissibility of previous similar conduct in certain cases.*
10. *The fairly recent innovation of Pre – trial Reviews and the process of Autrefois Acquit and Autrefois Convict.*
11. *The compilations of introductory, intermediate and final reports to the Director of Public Prosecutions.*
12. *The creation of schedules, symbols and charts affecting various aspects of suspected involvement with each other, the vehicles used, foreign currency exchanges and Incidents of thefts etc, etc.*
13. *Communications- correspondence, telex and telephone with witnesses, Police Forces, shipping agents, Interpol, solicitors and the D.P.P. etc.*
14. *Forensic science – continuity of evidence and transfer of exhibits between forces and documentation.*
15. *Correlation of over 190 exhibits and security thereof. Appointment of an exhibits officer and compilation of charts relating to incident, exhibit and accused.*
16. *The organising of witnesses in anticipation of and the progress of a trial and maintaining track of foreign seamen abroad, through Interpol and shipping companies.*
17. *The making of arrangements for foreign witnesses to be flown from Greece, Brazil, Hong Kong, Taiwan, America and Korea.*
18. *Similar arrangements made through the Greek Embassy by means of explanatory letters.*

19. *Accommodation, subsistence and witness fees for the witnesses.*
20. *Costs in Criminal cases, whether during or connected with the prosecution or otherwise.*
21. *"Attached" officer assistance from other Forces*
22. *Organisation of initial, intermediate and de – briefing conferences.*
23. *Maintaining or continuation of liaison between Forces.*

All the above matters require to be enlarged upon and it is my intention in the near future to provide a separate paper covering those and other associated subjects.

The officers mainly concerned in the investigations connected with Operation Cabinet, are, with the exception of myself, in reverse order of merit, as follows: -

DETECTIVE CONSTABLE JOHN RODNEY BRADLEY – *British Transport Police, stationed at Grimsby.*

He was on attachment to this office for several lengthy periods of time. During those periods, Detective Constable Bradley proved to be of outstanding ability and his assistance in the actual arrests and interrogation of the offenders, the collation of the exhibits found in the respective premises searched, the obtaining of documentation from various Banks and Building Societies in this area, his willingness to assist in other matters connected with this case and the subsequent preparation of the evidence relative to the above matters, proved invaluable. It naturally followed that because of his involvement he would have been one of the principal witnesses in the case, had he been called to give evidence.

I suggest a letter of Merit be sent on his behalf to his Chief Constable, Mr Ogram, informing him that he, Detective Constable Bradley, was one of the officers especially commended for his work by Judge Lawton.

EX DETECTIVE SERGEANT KENNETH CANDLER, *now serving in the I.C.A.C. Hong Kong.*

With Detective Constable Kenyon, Detective Sergeant Candler commenced the initial enquiries which eventually led to Operation Cabinet, as we know it today.

The initial enquiries were to be the foundation stone of all that later transpired. His diligence and accurate recording of events up to the time he resigned from the Force, set then pattern of a continuing and successful process of recording incidents throughout the United Kingdom and Continental Ports. From such recordings and following his joint discussions with Ex Detective Chief Superintendent Irvine, Detective Constable Kenyon and myself, the original schedules and symbols identifying various incidents were created.

Detective Sergeant Candler's diligence and effort played an important part in the construction period of Operation Cabinet and he too, had been required to give evidence, would have been one of the principal witnesses.

I suggest a letter of Merit be sent to the Director I.C.A.C. informing him, that he, Kenneth Candler, was one of the persons especially commended for his contribution to this case by Judge Lawton.

DETECTIVE CONSTABLE LESLIE EVANS

As the progress of Operation Cabinet had reached the stage where it was necessary to provide detailed and accurate charts and files of statements showing: -

a) Lists of evidence to be served.
b) Statements to be read in conjunction with the ` List of and index to statements of persons not tendered`.
c) Statements to be read in Conjunction with the `List of and Index to Unedited Statements not Tendered`.
d) Charts showing the relevance between the `Foreign Currency` exchanges by the seven accused and the incidents of crimes.
e) Charts showing all Foreign Currency transactions made by the accused.
f) Ordinary bank transactions.
g) Availability of witness charts.

I selected Detective Constable Evans to undertake these soul-destroying tasks. It goes without saying that whilst he could not do it alone, it was his diligence, his painstaking attention to detail and his all-round conscientious checking and re checking to ensure everything was correct, that satisfied the close scrutiny of the prosecution and defence counsels alike, without question. He was responsible for the 190 exhibits and had the case gone to trial would have been the exhibits officer.

Detective Constable Evans was also named by Judge Lawton and I suggest consideration for Meritorious recognition be given to Detective Constable Evans for his work.

DETECTIVE SERGEANT JAMES ANTHONY WRENCH

Has been involved with Operation Cabinet since its inception. As the Criminal Intelligence Officer, he was initially involved with the collation and dissemination of intelligence which helped to form the basic foundations of Operation Cabinet.

Throughout the whole of the enquiry he has maintained a liaison with many Forces. His `back room boy` support throughout these protracted enquiries, whilst not outwardly apparent have been a source of reliability without which no case could succeed.

He has been responsible for the dissemination of 52 bulletins regarding `Cabinet` alone. His contribution and natural cheeriness, particularly when sometimes there appeared to be an unsurmountable problem has been an inspiration throughout to all concerned.

Detective Sergeant Wrench was also named by Judge Lawton and I suggest Meritorious recognition be considered for his contribution to the success of this case.

DETECTIVE CONSTABLE PAUL KENYON

It is impossible to pay this officer adequate accolade for his dedication in this case. His naturally excellent memory for times, dates, incidents, cars and persons involved and witnesses concerned, eliminated constant recourse to search through the files and other material.

Detective Constable Kenyon began the initial enquiries into the activities of the suspects concerned and he established the links of those activities with other ports, which following consultations, led to the first conference of `Operation Cabinet`.

He made himself familiar with all the suspects and their associates and supplied totally reliable information concerning them, which, apart from Operation Cabinet, led to the arrest of Three suspects in Amsterdam, and Three suspects in Vancouver. The information, mainly gathered by Detective Constable Kenyon was supplied to the secretariat, Interpol, Paris, at their request and was later published in their International Green Warning Notice.

His contributions in creating the Operation Cabinet filing system of over 1,020 incidents, the compilation of evidence, the schedules, lists and charts is but a small portion of his total involvement in this case.

It was his zeal in the pursuit of evidence which led to the hitherto untapped source of information and evidence from Banks and Building Societies and played such an important role in securing the convictions of the Seven accused.

Detective Constable Kenyon has unswervingly given of himself in terms of time and no little personal expense, and of effort. His dedication to this case, to this Department and to the Force is in my opinion unsurpassed. I am personally proud to have had him on the team during this most protracted and involved enquiry and it augers well for this Force that we have such an officer who can absorb such tremendous demands made of him.

Particular mention of Detective Constable Kenyon was made mention of by Judge Lawton. I have no hesitation whatsoever in requesting consideration be given him to Meritorious recognition for his outstanding diligence, initiative, and whole-hearted efforts, which were the main factors in bringing Seven incorrigible criminals to justice and a successful conclusion to this unique case.

For my own part in this matter, I trust it will be regarded that I led this enquiry in a professional manner and in the best tradition of the Police Service.

Several congratulatory letters from different police forces have been received and are being complied to the attached file in due course.

Subtd, to Chief Constable 24.2.1984

Signed

J Ralphson
Detective Chief Inspector.

A couple of weeks after the sentencing, Fred Bakker rang, suggesting there should be a debriefing conference to discuss the operation, the pitfalls we came across and lessons learned, etc.

I knew it was probably a waste of time suggesting to the Chief that we host this in Liverpool, at that point I suddenly had a brainwave, why not Amsterdam? So, I turned the conversation around on Fred by suggesting the Korps Rijkspolitie (Rijkspolitie te Water) host the conference. Fred was immediately in agreement. I pointed out one stumbling block we had in Liverpool, and that was getting the Chief to allow officers to attend, but suggested that once he had fixed a date, he should write to our Chief asking for our attendance, after all we had been the prime movers in this operation. Also, adding he suggest that we be responsible for co-ordination of the British contingent, which would possibly be some thirty officers, from various forces. Fred agreed.

We sat back and waited. About ten days later J.R. mentioned the Chief had received a letter from Holland asking for our attendance and assistance in arranging travel for the officers from the UK who wished to attend.

From what I gathered at the time; the Chief wasn't really up for the expenditure bit. Anyway, to cut a long story short, J.R told him straight that the operation had been run on a shoestring and he was, in his words, "fast reaching the stage of getting dismayed at having to wangle this and wangle that to get the job done," suggesting myself and Tony Wrench be allowed to attend. He also pointed out that Cliff Hardcastle at Hull had managed to arrange significant discounts for travel on North Sea Ferries to Holland. Furthermore, Fred had sorted a particularly good package with the Hotel Lancaster in Amsterdam.

After a day or so we got the news that Tony and I would be going.

I then set about contacting all fifteen forces and police departments involved. This amounted to over twenty officers eventually booking for the conference.

On 25th April 1984, Tony Wrench, and myself, together with a couple of other officers who had self-financed their trip, left Liverpool and drove across to Hull for the evening ferry to Rotterdam. We met up with the other officers at Hull, before boarding the ferry for the overnight crossing.

On arrival at Rotterdam the following morning, we were met by Fred Bakker and some Dutch colleagues who transported us to Amsterdam.

The conference was held in the National Police Force, Maritime Branch Building, Amsterdam and commenced at 10.15 a.m. There was a warm welcome to all by Colonel K. de Maat, Chief of the National Police, Maritime Branch.

Following a lengthy morning conference, where we discussed the achievements and stumbling blocks (of which there were many), we retired to our hotel in Amsterdam for the afternoon.

Gathering early that evening at the hotel, we were taken to a distillery for a tour and sampling of the Dutch national drink, Jenever, a type of gin. There followed a dinner at the National Police Force H.Q., Sarphatistraat in Amsterdam, which was a formal occasion, with wives of the Dutch officers and dignitaries attending. There was also a government minister present.

The head of the Dutch police welcomed us and thanked the British officers for leading the operation and the part played by everyone. I responded and thanked all concerned for their tremendous assistance throughout the operation and for the hospitality shown to our party.

The next day was sightseeing, followed by a return journey via ferry to Hull.

So, it was back to reality and back to general CID work, as the Cabinet office had been mothballed.

The DPP had stressed in a letter, to Mr Donaldson, that it was considered a General Conspiracy charge should only be used in exceptional circumstances, much preferring to see the use of an individual substantive charge, where evidence was adequate and witnesses available. I tended to agree on that but feared the same old problem would occur, that of being unable to get witnesses back from across the world for an individual case.

That year, J.R., Les Evans, Tony Wrench and I were awarded a Merit Award for our efforts. We all chose a carriage clock suitably inscribed and presented to us by the Chairman of the Police Committee.

Later that year J.R. attended a conference of the European Association of Airport and Seaport Police in Marseille, France, where he addressed the delegates on Operation Cabinet.

John wasn't one for mincing his words and the following is an extract of his speech given to the delegates at the Marseille conference, all of whom were senior ranking officers.

"Operation Cabinet had previously been mentioned at International and European Conferences of the Association of Airports and Seaports Police therefore the reason for this dismal lack of co-operation or indeed interest from Belgium, France and Germany is inexcusable and must be squarely placed at the door of the respective Commanding or Senior Officers of the police forces in those areas, some of whom may be present here today. I can only hope, having reluctantly drawn these matters to your attention, the situation will now improve and not merely be left to lesser ranks who, despite the lack of support from their senior officers, in certain areas, try desperately to cope with these problems at ground level.

In this respect, I suggest you give consideration to appointing official liaison officers based respectively in Le Havre, Hamburg and Antwerp, and other ports wherever you may think appropriate.

COMMUNICATIONS THROUGH INTERPOL

Representatives of Interpol based in London and representatives from the National Criminal Intelligence Service in the Netherlands attended the various "Operation Cabinet" conferences and were most helpful in a practical sense however, Interpol in general terms did not seemingly give due attention and lacked a sense of urgency to the several requests made of them – an example of this is when it was requested through Interpol that a Captain Takado, a Japanese master of a vessel berthed in Trieste, Italy be advised he was required to attend the Liverpool Crown Court, as a witness. The first reply from Interpol, received a few days later was "We have contacted the local police, the Captain was not on board but in any event, he does not wish to attend Court". Being aware of the nature of Captain Takado, we found it difficult to accept this and consequently requested that Captain Takado be seen personally. In the meantime, and through the good offices of a shipping company, a message was delivered to Captain Takado, a result of which he in due course, flew to England, gave his evidence which proved the offence, and led to a conviction. He returned to Trieste the following day. Some three days following the conclusion of the trial, a message was received from Interpol to the effect that Captain Takado was willing to attend Court. It is perhaps better I do not mention my reply.

There is no desire whatsoever to make ridicule of the honourable department of Interpol who are renowned for their splendid work, the point being made however is that no department is infallible and therefore it is sometimes vital to an enquiry that other means of communication are not only more expedient but essential and more productive. This is a decision to be made by individual officers in accordance with the merits of individual cases."

All went quiet regarding cabin thefts following the finalisation of the case. We had none worth mentioning. It appeared the operation had been successful.

I remember halfway through the operation, meeting one of the team. He said, "It's only a game, Mr Kenyon." I replied, "Yes, but it's one we intend to win."

Additional items

Front cover of the Amsterdam conference agenda, showing the Operation Cabinet logo, Courtesy of Fred Bakker

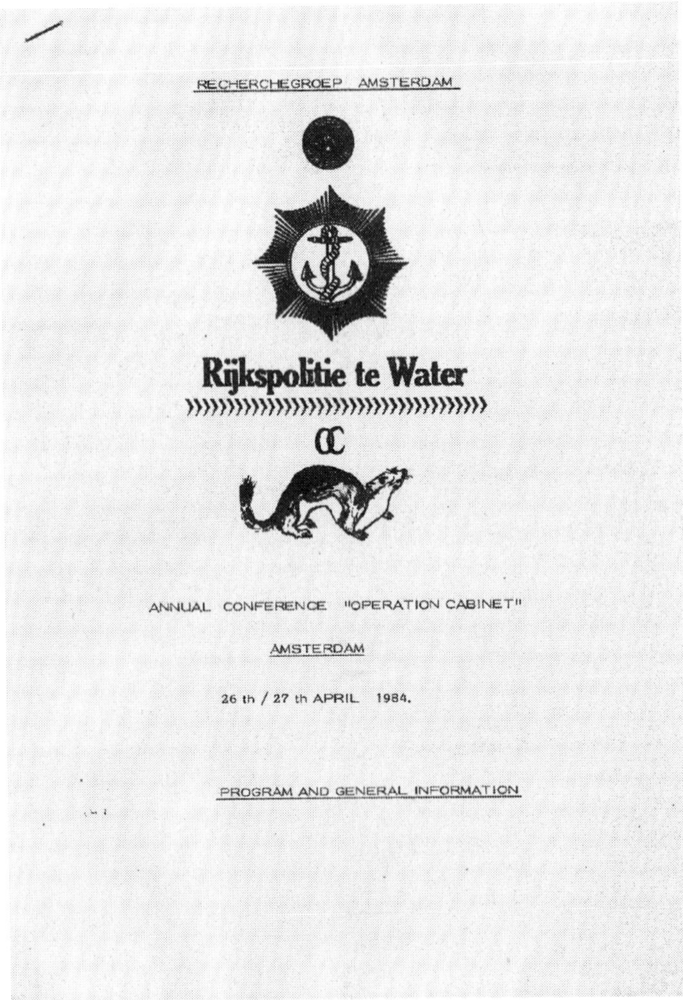

RECHERCHEGROEP AMSTERDAM

Rijkspolitie te Water

OC

ANNUAL CONFERENCE "OPERATION CABINET"

AMSTERDAM

26 th / 27 th APRIL 1984.

PROGRAM AND GENERAL INFORMATION

L to R

Commandant Fred Bakker, Gemeentepolitie, Rijkspolitie te Water, Amsterdam and Bill Thompson the Chief Constables driver .

Delegates Photo 1:
Amsterdam Conference
Gemeentie Politie, Rijkspolitie Te Water

L to R
2nd left *D/S Alan Brooker Interpol London. Cor Peeters Central Intelligence Unit, The Hague, Ministry of Justice. D.I. Cliff Hardcastle British Transport Police. D.C. Rod Bradley British Transport Police. D/S Rom Bosomworth Tees and Hartlepool Port Police. P.C. Kevin Barry Port of Liverpool Police.* Back Row 4th from left, *Tom Bartram Lancashire Constabulary.* Far right, *D/S Bob Wilson Port of Bristol Police.* Front kneeling, *The Author. P.C. Jack Socket Port of Liverpool Police. Commandant Fred Bakker Gemeentie Politie, Rijkspolitie Te Water. D/S Engen Van Dee Rijkspolitie. D.I. Dennis Ward British Transport Police C.I.S. H.Q London.* 2nd from right, *D/S Tony Wrench Port of Liverpool Police.*

See photo on next page.

Delegates Photo 1:
Amsterdam Conference

Delegates Photo 2:

At the Amsterdam conference on police launch outside the Amsterdam River Police H.Q.

L to R

D.C. Les Evans and his good Lady with J.R. upon his retirement in January 1985, note the carriage clock, which was awarded to him as a Merit Award, in relation to the work carried out on Operation Cabinet.

Credits

Photographs and documents:

Pg.7, Map: *Liverpool and Birkenhead dock estates by kind permission of the Mersey Dock and Harbour Company*
Pg.18, Photograph: *Liverpool River Police courtesy of Tony McDevitt Snr. R.I.P.*
Pg.88, Newspaper Clipping: *Excerpt from Daily Mail, referred to as 'The Bermuda Blab'*
Pg.201, Photograph: *John Ralphson, when a Detective Sergeant in the 1960s.* By kind permission of Roland Hatton
Pg. 202, Newspaper clipping: *Liverpool Port News article, February 1984,* courtesy of Mersey Dock and Harbour Company (Peel Management).
Pg.203, Photograph: *Eef Krabbendam* courtesy of Eef Krabbenham
Pg.222, Photograph: *Front cover of the Amsterdam Conference agenda, showing the Operation Cabinet logo,* Courtesy of Fred Bakker

Printed in Great Britain
by Amazon

58902757R00131